Stories

from my

Heart

JOHN POWELL, S.J.

Stories from my Heart

Foreword by Mark Link, S.J.

ThomasMore®

Allen, Texas

Send all inquiries to:
Thomas More Publishing
200 East Bethany Drive
Allen, Texas 75002-3804

Printed in the United States of America

Telephone: 877-275-4725
Fax: 800-688-8356

E-mail: cservice@rcl-enterprises.com
Web site: www.thomasmore.com

Library of Congress Catalog Number 2001086065

ISBN 0-88347-470-0

1 2 3 4 5   04 03 02 01 00

Contents

❧

"Prepare to have your heart touched, your soul stirred, and your future challenged. These stories will do precisely that. Picture yourself about to set sail on an ocean voyage with John Powell as your captain. You will sail to sixty ports and be entertained, inspired, and delighted at each of them. Enjoy your journey!"

—Don Driscoll, S.J.
Creighton University, Nebraska

Foreword

~~❧~~

What comes from the heart,
touches the heart. Don Sibet

This book is a beautiful example of what Don Sibet had in mind when he penned the above. It is much more.

It is having a gifted storyteller invite us into the sanctuary of his being and share with us stories that touched his heart and made him such a popular storytelling priest, teacher, and preacher.

John Powell is a storytelling priest.

Few have been blessed with such an artful ability to lead the community in celebrating who we are and what we are called to be. Elizabeth McMahon Jeep describes that calling this way:

> *There is a great similarity between the role of a priest in the Catholic community and that of a storyteller in an ancient tribe.*
>
> *Each bears official responsibility for handing on the stories which tell of the group's history and uniqueness, its folk wisdom and its vision of the future. They tell the people who they are, how they came to be a people, and how they are related to other peoples.* Liturgy 80

Father Powell is also a storytelling teacher.

He is able to do what the boss in Nikos Kazantzakis' *Zorba the Greek* wished he could do: "If only I could never open my mouth . . . until the abstract idea had reached its highest point and become a story.

"I once read that when *Reader's Digest* wanted to address a difficult topic, its editors waited until a story came along that dealt with the topic in a winning way. John Powell is able to do that. He knows what God tells Job in Robert Frost's "Mask of Reason": "Society can't think things out. It has to see them acted out by actors."

Finally, John is a storytelling preacher.

He does in a superb way what another masterful preacher, Walter Burghardt, urges all preachers to do:

The more we can turn to the picture language of the poet and the storyteller, the more we will be able to preach in a way that invites people to respond from the heart as well as the head.
Fulfilled in Your Hearing

Let me suggest a way to read *Stories from My Heart.* Put it next to your "prayer chair" and read only one story at a time. Read it the way Sydney Piddington read the few books he could smuggle into the Changeli prison-of-war camp in Singapore:

I spent three hours on two short chapters of Personal History by Vincent Sheean—savoring each paragraph, lingering over a sentence, a phrase, or even a single word, building a detailed mental picture of the scene. . . . And when finally I put the book down, my mind was totally refreshed.

That's the kind of book *Stories from My Heart* is. That's the way to read it and let it speak to your own heart.

Mark Link, S.J.

To My Dear Readers,

I remember when Grandpa and Grandma Powell would come to stay with us. I was only four years old, but I remember it vividly. I think that the thing we most looked forward to was Grandpa's stories. As the youngest of three children, I had the privileged position on Grandpa's bony knee. My brother and sister had to settle for the floor around Grandpa.

Since he was a man of great and deep integrity, he always began the same way. He asked us if we wanted a "real-life" story or a "homemade" story. If we had different preferences, Grandpa would ask us to vote. There is always a majority when three children vote.

Most of the following stories are real-life stories. A few of them, like "The Cliff" and "Rapunzel," are identified as "homemade" stories. They were composed by someone else. They are only narrated by me. I tried to live up to Grandpa's standards.

Stories. . . . I have found that we have a strong memory for stories. We also are very much moved by stories. The narrative style stays with us at a very deep level.

I have a secret, highly stylized method of judging "movies." The ones to which I give the highest marks are the ones I think about for days following the original viewing. So I am hoping that these stories move you as much as they have moved me, and that you think about them for days following the original reading.

And in years to come, when your children and grandchildren are adults, perhaps you will share these stories with them.

Remember me as loving you,
John Powell, S.J.

A Pair
of Silk Pajamas

⟿

Once upon a time I was teaching in a seminary. There was a hospital nearby. The seminarians who had gone into the local hospital for medical reasons returned with glowing accounts of a certain Sister. Later on I heard that this Sister was sponsoring a photo display of her works. I was amazed at her versatility and her talent.

One night I was called to the hospital. A nurse whom I had known was to be expelled from the nurses' program. She said it was a case of prejudice. It was for the wrong reasons that she was going to be expelled. She asked me to come to the hospital to hear the full story, and I agreed to do this.

After telling me the whole story, she volunteered to bring in one of her other instructors to verify what she had just told me. The instructor just happened to be the Sister about whom I had heard so much.

After the nurse left, the Sister and I chatted for a while. She asked me if I knew that she had been insane just three years before this. I was truly astounded, and asked, "Were you really insane just three years ago?"

She then told me about her stay in a mental institution, how she was catatonic, how the doctor told the Sisters that "she will just take up a bed the rest of her life." She stared hopelessly into space from her sickbed. However, her psychosis did have one extraordinary manifestation. She threw off all the bed clothing, including her hospital gown. A psychiatrist later told the Sister that she thought of herself as a thing, not a person. "We clothe persons, not things."

Then one day an orderly came into her room with a pair of brightly colored silk pajamas. She said in a motherly way, "You will look just fine in these." Then the Sister continued:

"She put her hand to my face, and I took the first step out of my catatonic psychosis, which I had inhabited. I held her hand against my face. It was then I realized that love does heal, that, as Augustine once said: 'Man is truly man's way to God.'"

From then on she made this the theme of life. In doing so she became a great woman herself.

Love is the only way to our human destiny and to the feet of God, who is love.

Carl Rogers' Gift

Carl Ransom Rogers was born on January 8, 1902, in Oak Park, Illinois. During his long and productive life, he had a considerable influence on the art of counseling. He insisted that the person in therapy has within himself or herself all the necessary tools to integrate themselves with the present situation. Thus, counseling was always "client centered."

One of his conditions for helping a person is that the therapist must experience an "unconditional, positive regard" for the client in therapy.

In other words, we all have the same problem, though the manifestations of each problem may vary. The basic human problem is low self-esteem. This low self-esteem may present itself in different ways.

A wise old priest once told me that if you cannot find something to like about the people who come into your life, you will not help them. So look through the personality before you and pick out something you can "like."

Rogers believed that the client in therapy has the responsibility to integrate the forces in his or her life for themselves. Consequently, it would be a serious mistake to direct them toward certain ideals or goals. The client must do this for himself or herself.

Having put in many hours of counseling, I now believe with Carl Rogers that I must have an unconditional positive regard, that I must find something I like in those who come into my life.

To do otherwise would be to worsen the problem that all human beings have: low self-esteem.

True love is and must always be a free gift.

Marilyn Monroe

❦

There are many plausible stories about the death of this diva. One of these stories is that she called a movie star and told him that she had just taken a lethal dose of sleeping tablets. In the words of Rhett Butler in *Gone with the Wind,* he replied: "Frankly, my dear, I don't give a damn." Marilyn threw the phone to the floor.

And so she died.

When her maid found her corpse the next morning, she discovered the phone lying on the floor beside the bed. The last words she had heard were: "I don't give a damn."

Claire Boothe Luce wrote an incisive piece in *Life* magazine, "What Really Killed Marilyn." In it she said that phone on the floor was somehow strangely symbolic of Marilyn's life, and of all human lives.

We all are looking and hoping that someone will just give a damn.

We are never less than individuals but we are never merely individuals. No man is an island.

He Preached
at His Own Funeral

❦

As far as I know, Frank Walter was the only Jesuit who preached at his own funeral.

When I came to my three-year study of philosophy, Frank Walter was the assistant minister of the community. This meant that he passed out lightbulbs, erasers, pencils, etc., to the members of the community. If it sounds like an unimportant job, given to someone as "busy work," it was just this. Frank Walter spent many years at this.

Later, I saw Frank at the university where I was teaching. He came there to make his annual retreat.

When he died, no one was assigned to preach at his funeral Mass. Instead, out over the crowded chapel came the voice of Frank Walter. It was played over an audiocassette which Frank had recorded in advance.

He expressed in his funeral sermon, among other things, his wonder that the Lord had loved him so well, and was about to give him eternal life. My mind went back to the philosophate and to the office of subminister, at which Frank Walter toiled so selflessly and quietly.

Every time I look at Frank Walter's obituary picture, I think of the saint of humility and faithfulness, Saint Alphonsus Rodriguez. For forty-six years he was assigned to tend the door at Mallorca. One of Alphonsus's biographers says of him: "Externally his life had nothing extraordinary or remarkable about it. He fulfilled his monotonous job with uncommon fidelity and humility and thus became a saint."

I am reminded too of the poem about Saint Alphonsus by Gerard Manley Hopkins, who pictures the great and famous of the day, whose names and reputations we have forgotten:

". . . while Alphonsus opened the door."

". . . while Frank Walter dispensed erasers and lightbulbs. . . ."

When we see our Christian lives in the perspective of the gospels, faithfulness to God's will is the only real, eternal crown of success.

My Early Education

❧

I didn't want to go to school at all. Actually, the competitor in me wanted to go just to be UP to my older sister and brother who were already in school. But another part of me wanted to stay home with my mama. Just the two of us had such a nice little world together. But the day finally came for me to start school. My kindergarten teacher, Miss Ford, once said to me years later that I was the "shyest little boy" she ever taught.

School was a wholly new and strange experience for me. It wasn't like my mama's kitchen, or Independence Park where we played right across the alley from our house. And it was very different than going to our summer cottage up in Waterford, Wisconsin. I knew all those places well and the people were all familiar to me. But school was different and all the other kids were different too. Some of them had parents who came from other countries and some of them even celebrated different holidays.

But as I gradually got to know the other kids, the teachers, and the school, I felt more at home in this bigger world. It even became exciting to learn about things that were new to me. Miss Smythe read to us kids, and so we heard about things all over the world. Each story made me want to hear more. I especially enjoyed reading class because I learned about so many other kinds of people. History class was another favorite because I learned about the world beyond my own little street. I had no idea there was so much life going on beyond Hamlin Avenue.

Pretty soon the competitor in me was unleashed, and I was volunteering to read and even be an actor in the little plays we put on. I learned to love school. Every day was a new adventure for me and each year seemed better than the last.

The Rosary Priest

I received an unexpected visit a number of years ago. It was from the famous "rosary priest," the late Father Patrick Peyton. When he first entered my office, the thing that most surprised me was his size. He was a tall man. The second thing that surprised me, I should say disarmed me, was his humility. He kept saying how nice it was of me to see him. I tried to tell him that his visit was an honor to me, but he would have none of that.

He had come to this country from Ireland, shortly after he had entered the Order of the Holy Cross. Perhaps it was his arduous trip to the United States, but he contracted tuberculosis shortly after his arrival. In those days, we had none of the antibiotics that control this disease, so Patrick Peyton was put in a sanatorium.

There, during one of his visits to the chapel, to the Blessed Sacrament, the Holy Spirit spoke to him:

"Patrick, you are called to start a radio program, to include all the well-known Hollywood movie stars. Your theme will be: 'The family that prays together, stays together.'"

Imagine, if you can, a young Irish-born priest being told that. Patrick was completely overwhelmed with the task laid before him.

His response to the challenge was: "I can't, Lord, but you can." All his hope and trust had to be confided to Jesus. It is a lesson for us all. After telling me this he gave me a rosary, and left.

When we come to that point of time in our lives when God wants us to do something specific, he will nudge us with his grace.

John of the Cross and Charley Sullivan

❧

I was riding in Charley's car, on our way to one of his missions in the country where I was to preach. I told him a story I had recently read in a life of John of the Cross.

It seems that John was incarcerated by his fellow monks, who believed that John was a bad influence on the monastery. He was even scourged for his supposed errors.

Then, as I recall, the Lord appeared to him and said: "John, you have borne all this with a true spirit of forgiveness. Anything you ask shall be granted to you." And the little monk said in reply, "Lord, that I may receive more humiliations for you."

I half expected that Charley would be as impressed by this as I was. Instead, he said, "What a terrible thing to ask for."

I asked, "What would you have asked for, Charley?" He said simply, "That Jesus might be loved by all, and that we might love one another."

I said to myself silently in the night as we drove along, "I will never tell the story of Saint John of the Cross without telling the story of Charley Sullivan.

(Charley Sullivan recently died.)

Saying "Yes!" to God's gift to love and life means choosing love as a life principle.

Michelle's Two Lives

❧

O nce upon a time, I was giving a retreat to high-school girls. A petite girl came in to see me. She asked if I was familiar with Our Lady of the Angels School in Chicago and the fire that had occurred there. When I nodded that I was, she showed me the scars on the lower part of her leg. "I was in that fire," she said.

"The nun who was teaching us told us to jump out the window to the school yard. Unfortunately, I was too small, and it was a struggle for me to climb up high enough to get to the window. Just then a larger girl looked back at me. She was almost out of the window, but she came back and lifted me up. When I looked up from the school yard, I saw only flames coming out of the window of our classroom. She had died in the flames, after saving my life.

"I have always wanted to do something good with my life, but since that day I have wanted to do something good for her, too."

It is my hope that she will succeed for both of them.

I might even ask if there is any person or cause for which I would give my very life. "No one can give a greater proof of love than by laying down his life for his friends." (John 15:13)

Mike Gold

Mike Gold was a Jewish man. He once wrote a book called *Jews Without Money*. At the end of his life, he had no money, and ate every day at Dorothy Day's center for the needy. She was once asked if she thought Mike Gold would ever consider becoming a Christian. She responded by telling the following story.

When Mike Gold was a little boy, his mother solemnly instructed him not to go beyond these four streets. She did not use the world "ghetto" because little Mike would have never understood. Prejudice is funny that way.

At any rate, with this child's curiosity at full steam, one day he wandered beyond the four streets, where he was accosted by a group of "bullies" who called themselves Christians.

"You a Kike?" he was asked. Mike Gold had never heard the word before. So he said nothing. "C'mon, you are a Christ killer, aren't you?" came the further questioning. Since he had never heard these words before, he said nothing. He simply looked down. So he was beaten up and bloodied. In this condition, he returned home.

When his mother saw the condition he was in, she asked him, "Mikey, what happened to you?" Again he did not answer because he did not understand. So she bathed her little boy and took him in her arms while she sat in a rocking chair.

Then he put his little bruised lips to her ear and asked, "Mama, who is Christ?"

"No," Dorothy Day replied. "No, I don't think he will ever become a Christian."

It is so much easier to love the God I don't see than the neighbor I do see.

Our Lives Are Shaped . . .

O ne of the many poster sayings that I am given credit for is not really mine. It reads: "Our lives are shaped by those who love us (and this next part is mine) . . . and by those who refuse to love us."

The first part of the quotation is from Lillian Roth's biography, *I'll Cry Tomorrow*. She had been an actress, a dancer, a movie star, and so forth. But she wandered into addiction and several marriages, and was dying in the gutters of this world. Then suddenly she emerged. She was on her feet again. When asked how she managed this, she replied: "Simple. I found someone who loved me."

At this point, she uttered the now famous words on my poster: "Our lives are shaped by those who love us."

Is this true?

Certainly, this has been my experience. Of the thousands who have sat in front of me during classtime, it is my judgment that those who were best adjusted were unconditionally loved by their parents.

The less well adjusted were the children of divorce. It was my reasoning that they knew their mothers and fathers had pledged undying love to each other "until death do us part." But they hadn't seen it through. The children of this experience may well presume that their parents' enduring love for them is just as fragile. Their parents, they reason, will not see that through either.

In the end, as Erich Fromm says in his book, *The Art of Loving*, they feel used, not loved.

Our lives are indeed shaped by those who love us . . . and by those who refuse to love us.

There was nothing I had to do. I didn't even have to be good. I just had to be myself. I was simply loved.

Rapunzel

This is a fairy tale . . . a Grimm fairy tale, somewhat adapted.

It seems that, once upon a time, there was a young girl named Rapunzel.

She was imprisoned in a tower by an ugly old witch, who was very repulsive. The old witch constantly told the young and beautiful Rapunzel: "You're just as ugly as I am, Rapunzel!" Since there were no mirrors in the tower, Rapunzel was sure that she was ugly. She never tried to leave the tower, fearing that her ugliness would drive others away. (This was the strategy of the witch: to keep Rapunzel a prisoner of her own supposed ugliness.)

And it worked . . . until . . .

One day Prince Charming rode by on a white horse, while young Rapunzel was leaning out of a window of the tower to get some fresh air. They smiled at each other, and it was love at first sight.

Rapunzel threw her long golden tresses out of the window (the ends, of course, remained attached to her head) and Prince Charming, having been a Boy Scout, wove them into a ladder and climbed up.

When their eyes were only inches apart, Rapunzel saw in the glistening eyes of Prince Charming that she was beautiful. So they promptly parachuted out of the window of the tower and lived happily ever after, with a few minor incidents brought on by the old witch.

Moral of the story: We all need the eyes of another to see our own beauty. As the song says: *You're Nobody Till Somebody Loves You.* Question: Do my eyes feed back to the others around me their beauty?

*W*hat I am, at any given moment in the process of my becoming a person, will be determined by my relationships with those who love me or refuse to love me, with those whom I love or refuse to love.

The Banister

❧

I used to carry my dear little mother up and down the stairs of our home in Chicago.

Mother had an incorrigible habit of hanging on to the banister, which prevented us from moving. When I would remind her of this she would look at me plaintively and say: "I'm afraid you'll drop me."

Whenever she said this I promised her that I would indeed drop her there and then. So she would let go for a step or two. Then the same dialogue would be repeated after another two or three steps.

One day it occurred to me that this was ironically symbolic of my own surrender to God. I was holding on tightly to some vaguely known banister, for fear that God might somehow drop me.

There are many banisters in my life. I must gradually try to sort through my own soul to find out what it is that is keeping me from a total surrender to God.

The old faith must die, eaten away by doubts, but only so that a new and deeper faith may be born.

The Cliff

⁓

This is just a story that someone made up, an illustration.

It seems that there was this man who was walking in the countryside. He accidentally tumbled off a cliff. He then grasped for anything he could reach and found that there was a tree root growing out the side of this cliff. So he grasped that mightily. And then he prayed:

"Oh God, help me," he cried out loud.

Suddenly, he was aware of a presence . . . and a question. God had come with his own question, to deepen the man's faith.

"Do you really believe in Me?"

"Oh, yes," responded the man fervently. (It has been said that there are no atheists in foxholes.)

"Then you believe that I can help you?"

"Oh, yes," replied the terrified man.

"So you will do whatever I tell you to do?"

Oh, indeed I will."

"Then . . . LET GO."

Some joker has added this line in the mouth of the man clinging to the tree root. "Hello. Is there someone else up there?"

I must get to know myself better, to find out how I would have reacted.

(Probably by doubting that I really heard the voice of God.)

Jesus urges us to ask and to keep asking. The rest is up to God.

In God's Own Time

∽

There was a Jesuit seminarian named Mike. After thirteen years in the order, he was close to ordination to the priesthood. Then his vision became blurred and generally his nerves seemed tight. He reported this, and was sent to a doctor.

The doctor, after examination, prescribed a relaxant which by a biological irregularity became for Mike a stimulant. He returned to the same doctor who decided to "double the dose." When Mike's vision became still more blurred and his nerves more edgy, he was invited to a conference with the rector of the seminary. "I don't know how to tell you this, Mike, but I think it is the will of God that you not be ordained this year."

He had always been an ideal seminarian, seeking only to do and be whatever God wills. So Mike quietly left the office of the rector and went silently to his room. Then he decided to tell God what he really thought. So he knelt by the side of his bed. There he thrashed his arms down on the bed and cried out, "You can't do this to me. I've offered You my whole life, given You the best years of my life. You can't do this to me. I am within arm's reach of ordination and You snatch it away, my life dream." Mike reported that the last time he thrashed his arms down on the bed, he silently moaned, "But you can do this. You are my God. You can do anything You want with me."

He added, "And this was the deepest peace of heart that I had ever experienced."

After the physician discovered that the relaxant was a stimulant, Mike was ordained the following year. But this very hidden drama will always be a part of his life as he continues to seek to do the will of God.

The great and infinite God asks a very limited and finite you and me: "Can you—will you—trust me?"

Rosie

❧

I used to give retreats to married couples. It always takes a "celibate" to do so. At any rate, I spoke to a couple who lived at a distance of seventy-five miles from the seminary where I was teaching. I was very impressed when this couple called the seminary and asked me if I would talk to their daughter Rosie. "Of course," I said. And so, the following weekend mother, father and their eighteen-year-old daughter appeared in the doorway of the seminary. After the introductions, the father began in a loud, "General Bullmoose" voice, "This is the kid. Do you want to hear her latest?" I quickly replied, "No, at least not here in the doorway nor from you." "So what do you want me to do?" the father asked. "We have some beautiful gardens outside. Why don't you and your wife take a tour of them?"

While mother and father were touring, daughter and I went to a visiting parlor. This time she began: "Do you want to hear my latest?" I interjected, "I'm dying to." So she told me about chugging (drinking down) a whole bottle of vodka.

I asked in amazement: "So what happened?" She answered, "I dunno. I went out. They had to get a doctor to revive me." At the end of our conversation, she asked if she could come again. Since there is nothing happening every minute in a seminary, I answered, "Yes, of course." As they disappeared I thought to myself, "At last, my charm is getting to her."

She did come back, and back and back. Every time I saw her, I liked her less. She was so self-centered. I remember well the day she came to the seminary with dire threats. She was determined "to git 'em." When I asked who it was she had in mind, she answered that her mother and father were the objects of her hatred. "They wouldn't let me use the family car last night to go to the Dive."

I had heard about the Dive. The local physician said he stitched up faces every Saturday night, faces which had been cut by the bottoms of broken beer bottles.

I thought it was time to intervene. So I said emphatically, "If I were your mother or father I would not let you go to the Dive either." "Oh, git off it!" (I had heard that so many times before. Every time I tried to get out my portable pulpit, she had told me to "git off it!")

On one occasion, I remember her telling me about her "boyfriend." Apparently, the poor fellow had never held a job. His only occupation was hustling in a pool hall. One night he came to Rosie's bedroom window with repeated cries of pain. Blood was streaming down his face, and onto his clothes. Either he had fallen down on his face, or he tried to hustle the wrong person in the pool hall. He couldn't remember which, so drenched was he with alcohol.

Anyway, Rosie drove him to the hospital, where doctors cauterized his wound. Tubes were put in both his nostrils, which in his drunken stupor he tried to pull out. So his hands were put in restraints and tied to the sides of his bed. Of this poor boy, Rosie said, "He looked just like Jesus

Christ on the cross." It was the first time she had mentioned Jesus Christ reverently.

I took the occasion of her sworn vengeance on her mother and father to remind her that what she needed was a "Copernican Revolution." She needed to find out that the whole world doesn't revolve around her but that she is supposed to revolve around the world, in acts of kindness. She grabbed at her books (I admit I wondered what she did with them) and stormed out, with me following saying, "Think about it, please."

About a month later, a psychiatrist came to the seminary to talk to the seminarians. I cornered him after his presentation, with an offer of something tall and cool to drink. (I knew it was kept in the infirmary "for medicinal purposes only.")

When we were settled into the infirmary, I asked him, "How do you teach people to love?" He answered: "Love isn't taught. It is caught. But no good psychiatrist ever answers a question without asking one. Why are you asking such a question?" So I told him all about Rosie, and the Copernican Revolution I had suggested.

"Well, to begin with . . ." the doctor replied, "first, you do not teach love. Love is a decision and commitment. A person has to decide to love, and then commits him or herself to the best thing for the one loved. Secondly, you did this girl much harm. She came out from behind her protective wall to you because you told her that her father, who taught her to hate herself, was wrong. You did this when you invited her father and mother to tour your gardens.

The psychiatrist continued, "I would bet my medical degree that when the emergency room doctor was reviving her from her alcoholic stupor she was saying somewhere deep inside herself, 'Oh, let me sleep. Let me die.'

"In the end, you told her that her father was right, that you agreed with him."

"Oh," I exclaimed, "I never said that!"

"You didn't have to. When you tell a person, 'You need a Copernican Revolution,' do you have to add: 'I don't like you either. Your father was right'?"

Then the doctor asked me a question, which I have repeated to myself countless times. "Did you ever have a toothache?" "Yes, of course I have," I answered. And he asked, "Whom were you thinking about at the time?"

"Any dentist," I said. "Anyone who can get me out of this pain."

"And that is what the girl saw in you, a healer of the pain she had memorized so long. I'll bet you thought it was your charm. No, you were her dentist."

So I wrote Rosie a love letter. I asked her to come back to the seminary so I could say one thing to her. She decided to accept, and when she came, I put my arms around her. She stiffened. "What's this mean?" I said, "What this means is that I like you." She snapped back. "You don't like me." So we went to the visiting parlor and began again.

Rosie didn't change, but I did. I listened through her stories (without laughing or cringing). The visits continued. One day she came in and told me she had been to confession. Then I asked, "How much do you drink these days, Rosie?" "Oh, I don't drink no more," she answered. (She dropped her boyfriend, and later married a very nice young man.)

For a few years I got pictures of her and her children. She was always smiling. And when I saw these pictures I thought to myself: "What if the psychiatrist had not come to the seminary?"

Can I trust you? How far can I trust you?
Will you understand or will you reject my feelings?
Would you laugh at me or pity me?

Little Miss Meanie

M any years ago there was a "drug" party at the university where I was teaching. One of the girls had a "bad trip." Rather than calling the police, her friend told her that, unless she sought counseling, she would "turn her in" to her parents, to the police, to anyone and everyone who would listen.

So one day she showed up at my office. Every other word from her mouth was an expletive. I must admit to wondering if she ate with the same mouth she talked with. She started off by telling me of her bad trip. She said a mountain was about to crush her. Her "friends" had to hold her down.

I was simply and totally amazed by her descriptions during each of our counseling sessions. It was in the springtime. When the students went away for the summer vacation, that ended our sessions. When the students returned in the fall, I asked her friend where she was. "Oh," the friend said, "she's been converted. She is now living with a Christian community out west somewhere, and writes letters like a nun."

I never anticipated this.

After several months had passed she came back to school to see her family and friends. She came to my office. She started out by hugging me!

When we were seated I asked her how her conversion had come about. (She was obviously very changed.)

I asked her if the counseling sessions had helped. She answered: "Oh, no. You offered me the velvet glove treatment. But the cook at a local chicken place, where I worked during the summer, had a different approach. More than once he said to me in his thick Appalachian accent, "My, you look unhappy, girl. Why don't you let Jesus Christ into your life? Let Jesus walk off the pages of your Bible and into your life?"

She continued: "Oh, cut the crap," I replied, "but unknown to him, I began to read the Bible every night. And one of those nights Jesus Christ did walk off the pages into my life."

I had been completely upstaged by an Appalachian cook at the chicken place. Me, with all my academic degrees (you may call me "Father Fahrenheit" if you wish). Out of the mouths of infants and babies . . . especially those with an Appalachian accent.

*W*ith the Lord's guidance and
your company, "every once in a while
there is a little tug on the string."

On to High School

～⌒⌐

My graduation from eighth grade was the highlight of my early education. I somehow managed to gather up all the honors summa cum "fraude," including "the outstanding boy" award. When my uncle drove me up to Loyola Academy, I was clutching my diploma and my "outstanding boy" award. We happened to meet the principal of the academy, and he said, "If you are the outstanding boy from your school, we won't have to give you an entrance exam." I was immediately relieved, as there was no possibility I could have ever passed the exam.

When the first English teacher announced there would be a diagnostic test so he could know where to start with us, I had immediate misgivings. These misgivings were confirmed when he asked what three kinds of sentences there were. I knew nothing of simple, compound and complex sentences. I remember putting down "long, short and medium." The teacher probably thought that he was dealing with a comedian, but I was utterly serious.

About midway through the year, it was announced that we would make a three-day retreat. When I learned that we were to keep absolute silence, I thought to myself, "You wanna bet?" I wasn't prepared for Charles Clark, who took the name "Dismas" for *himself, to honor the prison inmates he served when he wasn't giving retreats. Dismas is the name traditionally given to the "good thief," the man who was hanged next to Jesus at Calvary. The way Father Clark spoke to us and the stories he told were so riveting. He had a way of reaching right inside you and touching your heart. Each afternoon I returned to my home only to be dissolved in unexplainable tears. It was the first time I seriously considered the priesthood for myself.*

Years later, after my own ordination to the priesthood, I was helping at a parish in which Father Dismas Clark had just preached a mission. "How did he do?" I inquired. The young parish priest was almost ecstatic. He told me that the church had hung loudspeakers outside to accomnmodate the crowds. He also told me of plans to rent the local stadium in the event Father Clark would return.

Why do I tell you so much about Father Clark? Not to extol the man's nearness to God, but because he used stories, one after another. I memorized those touching stories, but could not retell them to the audiences I addressed. At the time, I feared they would sound too "corny." But, for me personally, it was like Grandpa Powell's bony knee again.

The Value of Trust

❧

In my junior year of high school, I had a driver's license. When I awoke one morning, I felt a little sick so I went back to my warm and inviting bed. When I got up at midmorning I felt good again, and remembered that our family car needed an "emissions" test. So I drove the car to an emissions testing center. When my mother was returning from the school at which she taught, the lady next door innocently asked her if the private schools were "off" that day. Unfortunately, she explained to my mother why she thought that.

Well, the long and short of it is that my mother would not write an excuse for me for the next day. She simply did not believe me. So I appeared before the desk of the man who took the excuse slips. He put out his hand, and I explained that I had no excuse, because "my mother doesn't believe me." He said surprisingly, "Well, I do." He gave me a pass to enter class.

That night, as I was drying the dishes, the phone rang. I answered the phone. It was the priest who had said he believed in me. I assumed he was calling to check my story. He asked to talk to my mother. Mother took the phone and was surprisingly gracious. All she kept saying was, "Yes, Father." She came from the phone and said to me, "I'm sorry. The priest who called from your school told me that he had no reason to mistrust you. You apparently have done nothing at school to betray his trust."

Naturally, I was amazed . . . and grateful. The fact that this story has stayed with me over the years is a testimony of how grateful and amazed I was.

It is important for all of us to experience the trust of another.

The only way one learns to trust . . . is to trust.

The Auction

A man and his son were great art collectors. They traveled around the world collecting art. They had originals by El Greco, de Maupassant, Gauguin, etc. They did this until the son was drafted into the military. That ended their search for art.

Then came the terrible telegram from the war department that the son had been killed in action. The telegram also contained this detail: "And it may be consoling to know that he died saving another man's life."

That other man later painted a picture of the son, and sent it to the father. It certainly was not a masterpiece, but it was recognizably his son. Then the father died, leaving behind his famous art collection.

The father had stated in his will that his art collection was to be sold at an auction. He had left specific instructions.

The auctioneer began with the amateurish painting of the son. There was a restless grumble throughout the crowd that had gathered for the auction. Finally, a man offered $9.50 for the painting of the son. It was all he had. "Going, going, gone for $9.50."

Then the auctioneer did a strange thing. He folded up all his papers, and announced to the bewildered crowd: "And that concludes our auction."

There were protests from the group. Finally, the auctioneer announced that this was expressly in the will of the father: "Whoever gets the painting of my son, gets all of my collection."

How true to life. Our heavenly Father has also said: Whoever gets My Son gets everything.

"If you remain united to me,
you will bear much fruit."

Dorothy Thompson

~~~

Dorothy Thompson was a writer, a syndicated columnist who did much freelance writing. I don't think she was much of a religious person. She was better known for her drinking.

Anyway, this same Dorothy Thompson was once interviewing a liberated prisoner from the Nazi death camp at Dachau.

He chilled even the veteran writer with his stories of the atrocities, performed by the guards and the prisoners. Finally, she asked him: "Did anyone remain human?"

His first answer was, "No, no one remained human." Then, after thinking for a moment or two, he said, "Yes, some did remain human. The religious people. They gave their meager rations to others who they felt were more in need. And they prayed for the rest of us."

Dorothy Thompson concluded her article-interview with these thoughts: "If you had gone to the homes of the few Nazis who were in charge, you would have found diplomas from the finest institutions in Germany. On their pianos, you would have found the greatest classical music, by the best-known authors.

"On their library shelves you would have found the greatest in literature.

"But I dare say the one thing you would not have found is a crucifix. The Jesus on the cross would have asked them: 'Why are you doing this?' I am beginning to think that when God goes all goes."

G*od sent his begotten son into this world,*
not to condemn it, but to love it into life.

Jesuit Friends

F rank had been a fellow seminarian with this other priest. They were stationed together in New York. Over the years, they had been the best of friends.

One day Frank heard the sirens of an ambulance in front of the rectory and went out immediately to see if a priest was needed.

He found his longtime friend lying dead on the asphalt of New York's street. He cradled the dead priest's head and shoulders in his arms for a long time, whispering: "You can't die. You can't die. . . ."

". . . I never told you that I love you."

The gift of love is the highest gift of the Spirit of God.

Charles MacArthur and Helen Hayes

~~

They were married, and that night on her pillow she found a string of peanuts, fashioned into a necklace. With the peanuts was a note which read: "I wish they were diamonds."

As you may know, both had very successful careers in the theater.

On their twenty-fifth wedding anniversary, on her pillow was a diamond necklace. With the diamond necklace was a note which read: "I wish they were peanuts."

Where your treasure is there your heart will be.

The Guru
of Communication

~❧

We were both invited to speak at a convention which was to last for a week.

It was the thesis of my talk that the people in a successful marriage must share all their deepest emotions or feelings.

The Guru then took the microphone with the express intention of setting me straight. In his talk he began emphatically insisting that he was married, and had greater experience than this little priest.

He went on to say that he himself edited his emotions, telling his wife only those feelings "which I thought she could handle." I remember sitting there quietly and asking: "Do you really decide which emotions she can handle or do you let her do this?"

The next day, we heard another married man say, "Martha can't be here for the whole of our convention. But she is arriving on Wednesday." On Wednesday, he introduced us to Martha. They hugged unashamedly and Martha took her seat in the audience. I thought to myself: Marriage works!

In his speech he remarked how he and his Martha at the time of their marriage had made the standard vows before God and a church filled with witnesses. Afterward, when they were alone, he told us how they had made more specific vows to each other. First on the list was a sharing of deeper feelings, with the "rider" that their deepest feelings should possibly wait sometimes for twenty-four hours. "If I come home with a deep feeling inside me and Martha has a crippling headache, my emotion can wait. But she will hear it the next day."

In some way, I felt vindicated by this subsequent speaker. I have often wondered if he meant to accomplish that.

Five years after the convention, the wife of the said Guru wrote and said he had left her in favor of a younger woman. (He was about seventy-two at the time.) The question I have lived with is this:

Did his marriage flounder because of what he confided to her of his deepest feelings or because of what he didn't confide?

The question of communication may be the most important question you or I ever consider.

Marshall McLuhan

Marshall McLuhan was "the expert" on communication a while back. He was a convert and a reader at Mass before he died. His pastor made a retreat which I had given, and told me this story of the Canadian, whose most famous book is *The Medium Is the Message*.

Preparing to read at Mass, the pastor looked over at him, and noticed little beads of perspiration on McLuhan's forehead. He asked, "Marshall, do you feel all right?"

"Yes, of course I do."

So the pastor followed up on his own question: "Marshall, you aren't nervous, are you?"

McLuhan answered: "Father, I am not going to read just any book. I am going to read the Word of God to His people. Of course I am nervous."

Help me to make this an act of love. Please don't let it be just another performance.

You Might Not Like Who I Am

❦

I was in my office, typing the final paragraphs of the manuscript, *Why Am I Afraid to Tell You Who I Am?* A friend came in for a visit. I was busy typing, so she asked: "What are you doing?" I told her what I was typing. She asked: "Do you want the answer?"

I raised my eyes heavenward, and told her that that is what the book is about.

So she asked again: "Do you want my answer?"

I responded, "Of course I do."

Then she said, "I am afraid to tell you who I am because you might not like who I am. What do I do then?"

In that moment I revised the manuscript to include my visitor's answer.

Strangely enough, when people say they have read this book, the part they quote is my friend's answer.

*I am not sure that I could even find
the words to share these things with another,
but what I am even less sure of is—
How would they sound to another?*

The Two Pigeons

⚬⟋

At a nearby university in the department of psychiatry, two hungry pigeons are put into separate cages. Neither pigeon has ever been in the cages before. The teacher explains that the desired conduct is to have the pigeons peck the black disk in the back of each cage. However, he explains, the cages are rigged differently.

In one cage, the pigeon is given a reward of a kernel of food by a mechanical arm whenever the pigeon pecks at the black disk. The instructor predicts that the pigeon will peck the black disk one hundred times in five minutes. It always happens just this way.

In the other cage, if the pigeon pecks elsewhere than at the black disk, he is given an electric shock. The instructor correctly predicts that the pigeon will suffer a few of these shocks, and then will sit in the center of the cage, with frizzled feathers, and not know what to do.

The instructor explains that it is the same way with human beings as with the pigeons. If human beings are rewarded for desirable conduct, you will see much more of the desired conduct. But if they are punished (the electric shock) for undesirable conduct, they will freeze and not know what to do.

If you will accept me wherever I am,
all my energies and desires to grow
will be released and energized.

A New Coat

❧

A nun told me this story of her mother. She always appeared at the family gatherings and all other social events in the same old cloth coat. So the kids chipped in and bought the mother a new fur coat.

At the next family gathering, the children noticed that their mother was wearing the old cloth coat. So they gently asked about the new one they had bought for her.

"Oh, yes . . ." said the mother. "I gave it away. A poor woman came to the door and her coat was so flimsy. So I gave her the new coat."

The children again asked tactfully, "Why didn't you give her this cloth coat?"

The mother ended the conversation with the remark, "We're supposed to give our best, aren't we?"

V*alues are caught, not taught.*

Fred Is Sick . . .

I was once at a party. The host (Fred) was perfect in every respect. He stayed on his feet, constantly asking others if they had enough to eat and drink. I was sitting next to his wife. She turned and whispered, "Fred is sick." I looked at Fred again. I saw only a smiling, friendly person, who seemed to be enjoying what he was doing.

When I could do it gracefully, I sidled up next to Fred, and asked him point-blank: "Are you feeling well, Fred?"

The answer surprised me. "No, I'm not feeling well. I had a kidney infection last week and I think it is recurring now."

So I returned to my place at the party, next to the wife of the host. I asked her how she knew that her husband was not feeling well.

She looked surprised, and finally said to me, "I am his wife."

I thought to myself. "They say love is blind. I think it is not blind, but supersighted." We often wonder about couples what she sees in him, or he in her. They obviously see what we do not. Love is not blind, but supersighted.

*L*ove is an art, not a science.

Loyola Love Story

❧

I recall being asked by our father provincial to go around to the various Jesuit communities in our province, to be part of a team of three to discuss, with the communities, devotion to the Sacred Heart of Jesus.

We came at last to my own community at Loyola University in Chicago. I don't know how to say this, but I do have a lot of mileage on my mouth, and am rarely nervous before a speaking engagement. But there I sat before my own community of about a hundred members, and I was nervous.

So I decided to put my own devotion to the Sacred Heart into action, and prayed (since I was the last of the three speakers I had time). I reminded the Lord that He had said: "Whatever you ask in My name will be given to you." I was asking for poise, which it is said you have to have, if you intend to influence the boys.

Nothing happened. So I came back to the Lord again. (He once said: keep asking. . . .) I reminded Him of his statement about giving any grace we asked for. But still nothing.

So I asked Him: "Are You trying to tell me something?" Since I decided I had said enough, I just listened. I think this is what I heard:

"You want poise so you can influence your own community. You want to show them how good you are. They don't need that. They need you to love them so they will know how good they are." (That's all she wrote, as the saying goes.)

I looked around the room. The first persons I looked at were the elderly. What is it like to be old, when you have to depend on others to do for you the things you used to do. The second group that caught my eye that night were the sick. What is it like to be sick, to wake up every morning with an ache in your bones (arthritis) or an ache in your guts (ulcers)? The third group that caught my eye were the alcoholics. There were about four or five members of my community who had this problem. All were members of Alcoholics Anonymous. They called it the "Irish virus" since they were all Irish. What is it like to be addicted? What is it like to celebrate Mass with grape juice? What is it like to stand up before a large group and say: "I am an alcoholic"?

The next group that caught my eye were the failures. I don't know how to say this humbly, but most of the things I have attempted have turned out well. What is it like to be a failure? One night one of the Jesuits who was present had prayed (out loud in a prayer group): "Lord, I don't expect success. Just don't let my failures hurt other people." What is that like?

I looked out over the same audience, and said under my breath: I'm going to love you. I don't know if I have truly loved you before. I am a nice, congenial guy in the community. I say "hello" to everyone as though I had just swallowed a greased billiard ball. But I mean it, I'm going to love you, to think about you and your needs.

When I returned to being me again, the nervousness had all left. The saliva had returned to my mouth, my hands were dry and warm again.

I think the Lord was trying to tell me all along that to think of yourself is the formula for tension and stress, to think of others is the formula for peace.

Under the crucifix there is the unwritten caption: "Greater love than this no man has. . . . Love one another as I have loved you."

The Chaplain's Companion

Once I was speaking at a university. I sat in the chaplain's room before the talk. I asked him who painted the trees on his walls. He modestly admitted that he did this. "I didn't know you were an artist," I said. To which he responded, "I'm not."

He continued, "You see, I had a near-death experience. After this experience I have been afraid of nothing. I figured that if I made a mess of this painting, I could splash more paint over my mistake."

"Tell me about your near-death experience," I asked.

"Well, I had bypass surgery. After operating on my heart, the doctors vainly tried to get it functioning again. They tried massage and electrical stimulation. Meanwhile, I was in a room with a man who did not identify himself, but I knew that He knew everything about me. He had his hand comfortingly on my shoulder. "We're not ready for the big trip yet," He said. I know now it was Jesus.

"When I came out of the anesthetic, the doctors were standing around me, perspiring profusely. 'How are you?' they asked. I replied, 'I'm fine.' (understatement) They said, 'We were afraid we had lost you.' So together we celebrated their successful surgery and my hidden experience."

I told this experience to Dr. Elizabeth Kübler-Ross, who said, "You should be out on the road telling others of this."

However, he elected to stay on at his university as a campus minister.

Sometime later, a student at the university was attacked and killed on her way to school. Father was elected to quiet down and reassure the campus community. He was alone on a platform with a microphone. Afterward, one of the young men on campus, well known for his faith, asked Father: "Who was that man standing next to you tonight, Father?" The priest was puzzled, "There was no one standing next to me." "Oh, yes, there was. I saw him with my own eyes."

"What did he look like?" The student described the same man who had placed his hand comfortingly on Father's shoulder during the operation.

"Why were you afraid? Didn't you know that I was with you?"

An Old Evangelist

~≈~

He was a very gifted preacher and teacher. He told me about his conversion to Jesus when he was young. He then hustled into his high-school classroom, and printed in large letters on the blackboard: JESUS CHRIST IS THE ANSWER!

When the bell that opened class had rung and the students poured into the classroom, he noticed that directly under what he had printed was another message: YEAH, BUT WHAT WAS THE QUESTION?

He was embarrassed at the time, but now in his mature years he reflected that Jesus Christ is the answer to all life's questions. If we have His vision, we will know the truth and the truth will set us free.

He explained to me that not all the answers are in the New Testament. The New Testament is not a catechism. That is what prayer is for: to look at reality the way Jesus does and then to act as Jesus would.

Our faith in Jesus is our comfort.
It is also our challenge.

Tommy

❧

T he first time I saw Tommy was when he entered my Theology of Faith class. Unfortunately, Tommy was an atheist or agnostic. He came into the classroom combing his long flaxen locks, which were down to his wrists. I immediately classified him under "S" (for strange).

In his nasally, whiny voice, he disagreed with almost everything I said. I think that the members of the class were more annoyed with him than I was. I personally found him a curiosity. I wondered a lot about his past. You see, I believe that the life script for every human being is written in the family.

In spite of this belief, that everyone makes psychological sense, I found Tommy like a case of athlete's foot. He didn't kill me, but drove me crazy with his various superficial objections.

At the end of the course, Tommy came up with his final exam. As he laid it on my desk, he asked in his usual whiny way: "Hey, Father, do you think I will ever find God?" I don't know why I do this, but on this one occasion I do remember that I tried a thing called "shock therapy." In answer to his question, I thundered, "NO." But just before he left the classroom, I said in a much lower tone, "You're not going to find God, but He is going to find you."

"Oh," he said. My great idea seemed to sail right over his head. I felt sure he didn't get a glove on it. And that, I thought, was the end of Tommy.

Then I noticed that he graduated. Like wow! I was happy that he had graduated because I would never see him again. I said a little prayer of gratitude.

Four months after graduation, I heard that Tommy was sick, seriously sick. While I was debating whether I should look him up there was a knock on the door of my office. I was surprised to see Tommy. He weighed about ninety pounds and his long locks were all gone. "Tommy," I said with sincere compassion, "I heard you are sick."

"I'm sick all right. In fact, I am a medical miracle. I have cancer in both lungs, my liver, and my kidneys. I have only weeks to live."

"Tell me about it, Tommy," I requested. To which he came back, "I'm sorry, but I get tired very easily. What I really want to talk about is the last day of class. Do you remember?" (I nodded "yes" and he continued.) "I asked you if you thought I would ever find God, and you said 'No, but God will find you.'

"What you didn't know is that I was not even looking for God. God would just come in and clutter up my life with rules. Besides, there was too much money to be made, too many women to be romanced, too many parties to be enjoyed, too many drinks to be drunk.

"With a couple of other graduates I formed a small company, and we were doing all right. Then . . . the doctors discovered that I had a suspicious growth. They took it out and said they would do a test of my lymph glands to discover whether the cancer had metastasized. I was alerted to this possibility, and when the doctors came into my room, I could tell by their faces that the cancer had in fact spread. They said they would immediately begin a program of chemotherapy.

"At this point, my life was on the line. I started praying again. I had asked God to wait in the wings until I called Him out. This was the time. I called God out but He didn't come. What I was doing was holding out my hoop and telling God to jump through it. God is apparently not a trained animal."

Then Tommy asked me a question: "Did you ever try something for a long time until you got fed up and you gave it up? One morning, that's how I felt about God and praying. I was 'fed up' even though my very life was at stake.

"I remembered something else from your class. You told us about your father with his DO NOT TRESPASS signs. I remember you said that the hardest thing to do in life was to go through life without loving. The second hardest thing to do was to go through life and, having loved, to keep love a secret inside you.

"So I went to my father, who was hiding behind his newspaper as he did every night. I said, 'Dad, I would like to say something to you.' 'Well, talk.' He lowered the newspaper just low enough to see over the top of it. 'Dad, would you just put down the newspaper? I want to tell you that I love you.' The newspaper just fluttered to the floor.

"My dad and I spent the whole night together, talking. We reviewed all the times I had smart-mouthed him, and the times he had grounded me. Early in the morning, he shaved and went off to work. But before he left, we hugged each other for the only time I can remember.

"Then I went to my little brother. I told him: 'Even though I made fun of you, wouldn't take you with me when

I went out, called you names, and so forth, I'm not going to be around too long. And when I am gone I hope you will know that I loved you.' My brother and I hugged each other for the first time meaningfully.

"Then it happened. God walked into my life. It almost seems that when you open your heart to others, God walks in through the open doors. Didn't Saint John write something like that, 'Whoever abides in love, abides in God and God is within him'?" (I remembered what Charles Peguy had once said: "If you try to go to God alone, He will ask you an embarrassing question: Where are your brothers and sisters? You didn't come alone, did you?)

"Oh, Tommy," I said, "you were a big pain in the back row when I had you in class. But now you are in a position to make it all up to me. Would you just come in to my present Theology of Faith class and tell your story? Just tell your story."

"Oh, wow! I was ready for you, but I don't really know if I am capable of facing your class. But I will let you know." He didn't make it, but at the hospital before he died, I did visit him. The last thing he said to me was: "You tell them for me. Will you?" So I have now told you, as I have told many people.

*C*hoosing love as a life principle widens the chalice of my soul so that God can pour into me his gifts and graces and powers.

My Seminary Years

❧

*M*y seminary training consisted of two years of novitiate, two years of juniorate, three years of philosophy, three years of regency, four years of theology, a year called "tertianship," and two years of studies in Rome. The novitiate was something else. I have detailed my experiences in a book called Touched by God. It was in the juniorate (the two years after the novitiate) when I learned that I could write. A classmate of mine had started the "Knights of the Inkwell." When these "knights" sponsored a writing contest, I won five of the seven awards. It occurred to me then that writing was possibly my best talent.

After regency (practice teaching) I entered the final stretch: theology. Somehow I knew that this was my field. When I told one of my teachers that I wanted to write a book about Jesus, he very politely told me that I should begin with an article or two. After I explained what I planned to write and why, he agreed. So I wrote my first book, A Stranger at Your Door. And it was published by Bruce of Milwaukee.

Theology did become my "field" and at the conclusion of my studies, I was sent to Rome and the Pontifical Gregorian University for a doctorate in theology.

I arrived just as Pope Pius XII had died and I attended his funeral. What I discovered in Rome was *that all human beings are very much the same, as witnessed by the following story:*

After my first year at the Gregorian, I toured Europe with an African priest, who was later to be a bishop, Father Pasu-Pasu. He was very large, about seven feet tall and 250 pounds. When the children of Europe gazed up at him, he softly greeted them. I should add here that he had his front two teeth filed to a point. It was the sign of his tribe back in Africa. When we got to Spain, an American boy insisted that we see a bullfight. So Pasu-Pasu and I found seats in the grandstands of the arena and waited for the event to begin. The bull was released, and four or five men put banderillas in its sides. With blood dripping from the wounds, the bull was sufficiently agitated and then the bullfighter named Gregorio entered the bullring. Pasu-Pasu looked at me and echoed my sentiments exactly. "Cruel, isn't it?"

Alberto and the Image of God

~⊙

We were in our last year of Jesuit training, called Tertianship. An important part of this year for me was that the community was comprised of Jesuits from the four corners of the world. We had a German, two Canadians, and the man about whom I wish to tell you. He was from a South American country, and in general a perky little guy. (I found out much later that he was a classical pianist.)

He was very cheerful, except when he was celebrating Mass. We "served" each other's Mass, and one time I was paired with Alberto, and noticed his morose manner during Mass. When we took a walk together later in the afternoon, I mentioned this to him.

He was so good and so honest. He immediately and openly acknowledged this.

"It is the country I am from," he said. "'My mother took me into a church when I was a little boy of four or five. She showed me the life-sized crucifix, with painted wounds. 'Poor Jesus,' she said.

"If a child cries at this point, it is a good sign that he or she is destined for the religious life. Most religion in my country is heavily flavored with this sadness. It almost seems that we have picked out only one of the aspects of religion and allowed it to influence all of our relations with God."

It sounds a little like Phyllis McGinley's poem "Who is God?" In it she humorously says that this depends on where you went to church last Sunday.

We find God in the joys of human love, in the exhilaration of a sunset, starlight, a heavy snow bending the branches of evergreens in winter, in a fireplace at the end of a perfect day.

The Popcorn Machine

∾

If we have been called to be fully human and fully alive, why did Thoreau say that "Most of us live lives of quiet desperation"? Why did Hubert Humphrey need to remind us that life is to be enjoyed, not endured? What is the significance of the *Talmud* telling us that every one of us will be called to answer for every legitimate pleasure that was not enjoyed? Obviously, something is missing from most lives. Somehow the light has failed, something has gone wrong.

In his verse, "Out of Order," Father Andre Auw records his reactions when he comes upon the scene of a young mother trying to explain to her four-year-old son that the popcorn machine cannot give out its contents.

> *"You can't get any popcorn, Child. The machine is out of order. See there is a sign on the machine."*
>
> *But he didn't understand. After all, he had the desire and he had the money, and he could see the popcorn in the machine. And yet, somehow, somewhere, something was wrong, because he couldn't get the popcorn.*
>
> *The boy walked away with his mother, and he wanted to cry.*

And, Lord, I too felt like weeping, weeping for people who have become locked in. Jammed, broken machines filled with goodness that other people need and want and yet will never come to enjoy because somehow, somewhere, something has gone wrong inside.

There is no learning to live without learning to love.

What Does Your Sign Say?

～๑

D id you ever play that party game in which you wore some name on your back, and you tried to guess what it said? Others who could see the sign were allowed only to say "Yes" or "No" to each of your guesses.

It has been forcefully pointed out to me that each of us has a sign which we carry in front of us. Everyone else can read the sign except us.

The sign may read: I'M NOT IMPORTANT. Or DON'T MESS WITH ME. Or I'M LONELY. I AM A FOLLOWER. WILL YOU FILL MY VOID? JUST TELL ME WHAT TO DO. Try to guess what sign others carry out in front of them. Then notice how everybody obeys this sign, treating them as unimportant, or as an intellectual, or perhaps as an emotionally explosive person.

It sometimes takes a long time to guess what your own sign reads. You almost have to deduce this from the way others treat you. Do they ignore you? Are others intimidated by you? Are you a leader or a follower?

I think you will conclude that you have personally written this sign and that it's what you show to others. It may take some time, but it will be well worth your while. What does your sign say?

T ry to learn who you really are
rather than tell yourself who you should be.

Dr. Paul Brand

❧

P aul Brand was a medical missionary to a leper colony. One of his many messages to us was: Love your pain. He explains this based on his experience as a medical missionary. He once said that we see lepers with missing fingers and even noses. We presume that it is the leprosy (Hansen's disease) that has done this, but we would be wrong in such a presumption.

It is rather that lepers have lost sensation. The Hansen's disease does this, it robs them of pain. They can touch a hot oven or pan without realizing that it is hot until a finger drops off. Or they can scratch an itchy nose and an infection sets in and the nose drops off. I think the purpose of Dr. Brand's advice, to love our pain, is obvious.

All pain is a teacher telling us something about ourselves. It may be physical, or emotional or actually spiritual. We can be sick, or suffer from a wide variety of feelings, or be without any real meaning in life.

Dr. Brand would tell us to love our pain, and part of loving the pain is to investigate its sources. Like the pearl of great price, we will discover something about ourselves. What? That is for the individual to decide.

Another doctor, Dr. David D. Burns, has written a book on the various sources of psychological discomfort. His book is called *Feeling Good: The New Mood Therapy.* In this book, Dr. Burns, who is a professor of psychiatry, discusses possible sources of human discomfort. It is well worth reading.

You see, I believe that 95 percent of human suffering is needless, if not neurotic. When someone beloved to us dies, we will never see that person again. This is real suffering. But the suffering of a guilt complex, anxiety over the future, or an inferiority complex, these we can do something about, and we should.

So, as Dr. Brand says, we should love our pain and investigate its sources, whatever they are.

The greater the distraction of pain, the smaller will be our capacity to love and care about others.

Enabling Versus Tough Love

❧

A priest once wrote in a journal for priests that he was an active alcoholic for many years. There were those days when he simply couldn't make it to class, but there were always members of his religious community who would fill in for him. They cleaned up his vomit, they put him to bed at night, woke him up in the morning. He had conscripted an army of "enablers" to help him keep drinking.

He was an excellent musician and was the type people wanted to invite to parties—as long as he could see the piano keys, which is to say, as long as he was sober.

He then wrote in his article about being confronted by another priest. It is said in the literature on alcoholism that one has to "hit bottom" before the person can rise again. But the technique called "confrontation" is often used. It raises the bottom one has to hit.

The other priest stood on the other side of his desk in his room and confronted him:

Eddie, you're a drunk. You have to do something about it or I will. I'll tell the head of your department, the rector of this community, everybody.

He concluded his article with the words: "Thank God, someone finally had the guts to tell me the truth. It was tough love at its best. I will forever be grateful to him."

Note: Confrontation in this story seems to work automatically. The fact is that most alcoholics resist the truth, so confrontation is best done by the family and those who know the drinker well. It should be rehearsed, and done under the guidance of a professional in this matter.

If you have tried and failed,
and you just need a hand in yours
in the darkness of disappointment,
you can count on mine.

People Are Like Flowers

❧

The veteran teacher surprised his class with their homework assignment. It was to find a little wildflower growing by the side of an obscure road, pluck it, and turn it in the sunlight.

Turn it, he continued, until you can see its full beauty, until you can see all the veins in its petals, until you can see the blossom and identify its shape and color.

When the students came back to class the next day, the teacher said simply: "People are like flowers." Their full beauty often lies unrecognized. Because of their location, they are often overlooked. No one ever looks quite close enough to appreciate them.

Unless you see something of this beauty, you will not be able to help them. You will overlook them just as everyone else does.

In a true sense, each one of us is a unique masterpiece of God.

A Man Named George

❧

W hile I was teaching, prior to my own ordination as a priest, I got to know an extraordinary man named George Sullivan. George had been a top-notch salesman in his younger years, but when he was thirty-five, George suffered a heart attack. The doctor forbade him to have sexual relations with his wife. When George was in his forties, he suffered cancer in his sinuses, and the surgeon had to remove his nose, substituting a prosthesis for it.

Because of the condition of his heart, George had to accept a sedentary job, dispensing checks to the city employees in a cage at city hall. Because of his prosthesis nose, George preferred to spend his free time at home playing cards. One afternoon, when we were at our usual Sunday afternoon card game, I asked George point-blank. "Did you ever feel sorry for yourself, George? Have you ever asked 'why me'?" I will never forget his reply. "These are the cards God has lovingly dealt me, and these are the cards I will lovingly play."

One night George's wife phoned me. She tearfully reported that George could not breathe, and seemingly was having another heart attack.

I immediately dropped all the things I was doing and rushed to their apartment. The ambulance driver was just getting ready to pull away, and when I tried to get aboard, he said that this trip was "only for family." I announced that I was a part of the family. I knew George would have wanted it this way.

George offered me his hand which I held on the way to the hospital, where he was pronounced dead. The paramedics had placed an oxygen mask over his face, and what turned out to be his last human act he winked at me. He seemed to know that everything would be all right. "These are the cards God has lovingly dealt me and these are the cards I will lovingly play." I used that quote at the end of his funeral homily.

Christians have always believed that this life is a mere dot on the endless line of our human existence.

Sydney Harris Learns a Lesson

Ᏸ

I wrote up this story in my book, *Why Am I Afraid to Tell You Who I Am?* It is based on a newspaper column of the late Sydney Harris.

The fully human person is an actor, not a reactor. Sydney Harris, the late syndicated columnist, tells the story of accompanying a friend to a newsstand. The friend greeted the newsman very courteously but in return received only a gruff and discourteous service. Accepting the newspaper that was shoved rudely in his direction, the friend of Harris politely smiled and wished the newsman a nice day. "Don't tell me what kind of day to have!" the newsman sourly replied. "I have other plans."

As the two friends walked down the street, the columnist asked: "Does he always treat you so rudely?"

"Yes, unfortunately he does."

"And are you always so polite and friendly to him?"

"Why, yes I am."

"Why are you so nice to him when he is so rude to you?"

Sydney Harris reported genuine surprise at the answer
to his question:

"Because I don't want him to decide how I am going to act."

Sydney Harris thanked his friend for the lesson in human
relationships as the two men continued down the street.

To thine own self be true.— Shakespeare

The Empty Chair

❧

I believe that the most determining thing about any human being is what he or she thinks about himself or herself. So I have devised an imagination exercise called "the empty chair." (I am sure I borrowed it from someone else, but I cannot remember who it was.) It is designed to help a person come into real contact with himself or herself.

As a part of The Fully Alive Experience, I gave a weekend presentation to various groups in the years 1977 and 1980. In Louisville, Kentucky, I directed "the empty chair exercise" to those gathered. About a month later, a letter arrived from one of the participants who wrote: "The empty chair exercise changed my life."

Briefly, the exercise asked the participants, after closing their eyes, to imagine an empty chair about six feet in front of them. The first of three persons to walk out of the wings of the stage and occupy that chair is someone well known to you: a member of your family, a coworker, a classmate at school, or someone that you know quite well or see quite often.

Look long and hard at this person. Does the person like you? Do you like this person? What is the outstanding thing about this person? Finally, you get to say one thing to this person without a reply. Something like, "Why don't you like me?" or "Why do you lean on me so much?" Or something uncritical. Then the person quietly leaves the chair and the center stage of your imagination.

The second person then walks out of the wings of the stage of your imagination. He or she is also a person well known to you. Again, you study this second person to see whether he or she likes you or not; also, whether you like this person or not. You get to say only one thing to this second person with no reply. Then the person quietly leaves the chair in front of you.

The third and final person to sit in this empty chair is YOU. You are face to face with yourself. Look long and hard to see if you like that person who is you, and see whether that person likes you. Again you get to say one thing to that person and then he or she quietly leaves the empty chair.

The letter from The Fully Alive participant continued: "The me I saw was a wimp. A real wimp. I was determined to please everyone and pleased no one. It was all just an act. My life had been a charade. I saw in response to your directives that I did not like myself at all. What I said to myself is simply: 'You are a wimp. You may have been brought up to be this, but it's time you did something about it. C'mon, grow up. Be true to yourself.'

"I can't say that I changed overnight, but it was a rude awakening. I have been changing. And you are right about the saying that people treat you as you advertise yourself.

"My message was: 'You count but I don't.' Now my message is: 'You count but I *also* count.'

"Thank you so much."

*W*ith the help of God and those who love us,
we can rewrite our "life script."

The Legend
of the Irish King

༄

I remember an Irish storyteller named Seamus McManus, who told me this story:

There was a day when Ireland was ruled by kings. The reigning king had no sons to whom he could turn over his empire. So he had his pages put this notice on all the trees: "If any young man has these two qualities, he should apply to the king for an interview, with the prospect of inheriting the kingdom. He should: (1) truly love God, and (2) truly love other human beings."

The young man who read one of these notices felt he truly loved God and others, but he knew at the same time he was too poor to purchase the clothes needed for an interview with the king. Besides this, he had no money for the provisions to travel all the way to the castle. After telling others of his dilemma, his neighbors provided the clothes and the provisions.

So the young man set off for the castle. However, just before he arrived, he encountered a beggar by the side of the road. The beggar extended scrawny arms in supplication. "I am hungry and cold," he said. The young man was so moved he gave the beggar his new suit of clothes and all his provisions. Putting on the rags of the beggar, he knew he had to make a decision.

He decided to go on to the castle of the king, where an attendant showed him in and had him wait for a couple of hours before he was finally admitted to the throne room.

He bowed low before his king, and when he raised his eyes, he was astounded. "You . . . you are the beggar I met on the side of the road. But you are really the king of this country. Why did you do this?"

The king, in his ermine robes and golden crown, replied: "I did this to find out if you really loved. You truly do love God and others and you shall be the next King of Ireland."

Thus far the words of today's holy Irish legend.

But I must ask myself: Would I have passed the Irish king's test?

The size of a person's world is the size of his or her heart.

The Nearsighted Boy

I remember a boy who could see only what was right in front of him. He had very little long-range vision. So he figured out life accordingly.

He reasoned that the teacher wrote on the blackboard so she could remember what it was she wanted to say. Why were street signs hung so high on lampposts since no one could read them that high? He reasoned that this was done so that the bus drivers who sat up close could call out the streets for their passengers.

Baseball he could not figure out. The batter could see the pitched ball only as it crossed the home plate. Not enough time. So he had no interest in baseball.

One day he went to an eye doctor who fitted him with the appropriate lenses for his vision problem. Then the doctor told the boy to look out the window of his office.

For the first time the boy could see expressions on the faces of those who passed by. He could see leaves on the trees. He could even see the sky and clouds. Wow! It was so exciting!

He was describing this to me and at the end he said it was the second most exciting experience of his entire life. So I had to ask, "And what was the most exciting experience of your life?"

He looked at me as though I should know. I didn't. "It was the day I first believed that Jesus loves me, and that everything in my life happens because He wills it."

I silently thought of Dag Hammarskjold, former Secretary General of the United Nations, who wrote in his book, "On the day I first believed, life had meaning and the world made sense."

Why isn't faith more exciting for me?

The Word of God which we accept in our act of faith is indeed very good news.

Growth Begins Where Blaming Ends

❧

This is a popular aphorism among psychiatrists—There obviously comes a time when we must no longer find fault with someone else (our parents, for example) and roll up sleeves to do a little work on ourselves.

Recently, I came across an example of the same, and wish to share it with you. A friend of mine, named Kay, was driving to the store. There was a sign of very small proportions that read: "No left turn here between the hours of 4 and 6." Kay innocently made a left turn there, parked, and entered a department store. A large officer came in later, and thundered: "Is that your car out there with license plates . . ." "Yes, it is, officer, did anything happen to it?" "Don't sass me, ma'am. You made a left turn back at the intersection. It is prohibited at this hour." "Whew! I thought something serious had happened," Kay responded.

At this, the officer called for back-up help, to protect himself against further violence by this mother of six. In brief she was cuffed, and taken to the station. There she was fingerprinted, strip-searched, and put into a cell. When I sought to verify the details, Kay made light of it all. "The arresting officer was a kid looking for a mother." "How did you know this, Kay?" I asked. "Well, he once slipped and instead of calling me ma'am called me MOM."

She thanked the female officers who strip-searched her, and the officer who fingerprinted her. "During Passion week, I will better understand how the innocent Jesus felt," she said.

In the end, a police captain straightened out everything, and Kay went on her way. When I asked her if she intended to sue the village in which this had happened, she said, "Oh, no, it was one of the best experiences of my life." Apparently, growth does begin where blaming ends.

The direction of your flight, the song you will sing, and the warmth you will bestow on this world are your responsibility.

It's All in How You Look at It

❧

I have been telling people that we make our own lives whatever they are because we make our own experiences which ultimately comprise life. "What you see is what you get." (One of my favorite expressions.)

For example, if I see a snake on my front lawn, whether or not it really is a snake, it IS for me. I immediately get a hoe and hack the creature into small pieces. I then go inside to drink something strong to settle my nerves. Only on the next day do I find out that someone else had left the garden hose on the lawn.

I am also fond of quoting that famous verse: "Two men looked out from prison bars, / One saw mud and one saw stars." In other words, whatever you see is what you get. Or two people who are thirsty see a glass half-filled with water. One says, "Water, at last." The other laments, "It is only half-filled." Two different attitudes.

I was driving along an expressway in Chicago when the car I was driving suddenly died. Everything went off: the air conditioner, the radio, etc. I didn't know about the "master fuse" at the time. In fact, the only thing I knew about cars were their colors, and I wasn't sure about some of them.

Anyway, I was able to pull the car off to the side of the expressway. I did know about raising the hood or the trunk lid. I tried to do this but the wind almost blew the hood and the trunk lid into Wisconsin. Chicago, I mused, is not called the "windy city" for nothing.

I looked to the west of the expressway only to see a steep hillside with a fence at the bottom. I prudently decided not to attempt the descent. I probably would have caught my trousers on the fence anyway. I also decided not to cross the expressway, since there were six lanes of traffic whizzing by. My mama did not raise a bunch of dummies.

So I started to hitchhike. I was wearing my Roman collar, so I thought it would be automatic. (You know, me and my R.C.) As the cars continued to whiz by me, I thought to myself, my mother said there would be days like this.

Finally, a small car pulled off the expressway, and the driver opened the passenger door. I was already aboard and had fastened the seat belt before he asked me if I wanted a ride somewhere. "Take me to a telephone," I nervously stammered.

About two weeks later, a young woman who types for me came to my office late. After apologizing for being late, she told me about how her car had broken down. It was the exact same place my car had broken down two weeks earlier. I immediately thought of the "Bermuda Triangle."

"So what did you do?" I asked, anxious to compare her experience to my own. "I climbed down the hill, went over the fence, and found a phone." "So how did you feel?" I asked curiously. So help me, she said: "Exhilarated." And so help me I said, "Oh, I hate you."

She had seen only challenge, and felt exhilaration. I had seen only danger, and felt panic. What you see is what you get. Two different attitudes, two different ways of seeing things.

The most important part of my vision of reality is the vision of myself.

Suicide by Drowning

৵৩

Years ago I wrote a little book called *Touched by God.* It was never on the best-seller list, and, in fact, it was not one of my own books that has sold all that well. But it has brought in more correspondence than anything I have ever written or done.

Most of the letters have had to do with a similar experience. Apparently, God has touched many others, too.

But one of the letters caught my attention and stays with me to this day. As I remember, it started out blandly. But then the person admitted that she had led an "evil" life. She admitted that she knew only one way to stop all this evil, and that was by suicide. But how?

The letter came from the southeastern part of the United States, and apparently she lived near the ocean. The author of the letter had decided on death by drowning. (It is one of the two ways I personally do not wish to die.) She had walked by the oceanside on numerous occasions, and felt that the ocean, like a mother, would rock her in its vast waves.

So, one morning, as soon as day had broken, she set out. As anticipated, no one was on the beaches. She walked along the sandy rim saying a slow goodbye to all that she had known. Suddenly, a loud, imperious but gentle voice told her to stop, to turn around and look down. After looking on the beach for an intruder and finding none, she did as the voice commanded her. She noticed only that the ocean had washed her own footprints away.

"I am calling you to live and to love, not to die," continued the strange voice. "Just as you see the ocean has washed away your footprints, so my love and mercy have washed away all of your sins. I am calling you to live and to love."

The author of the letter openly admitted that she had shared the experience with no one. For two reasons, she wrote. "The first reason is that it is a deeply personal matter, and the second is that my whole life is based on that one experience. I don't want someone to laughingly say, 'Oh, you just didn't want to die, so you made up that voice.'

"You see, I have put my life together again. Things began to fall into place after that. I am happy again."

I concluded my little book with the words: "This is my act of love for you, Dear Reader. Take it in gentle hands." She concluded her letter with almost the same words:

"And this is my act of love for you. Take it in gentle hands."

The "I" of God has been saying to the "Thou" of you and me an eternal "I love you."

Padre Pio

❧

Thirty-some years ago, I was a student in Rome, Italy. I was getting a doctoral degree in theology. During one of the summers I went to the Holy Land. It was quite an experience. But nights were a contest because I roomed with another priest who snored very loudly. On our return by boat we docked at the southern tip of Italy, at a city called Bari. Then we boarded a train for Rome. I was intently looking at the map, when suddenly I saw that we would pass through Foggia. I looked up from the map and said to my loud-snoring friend, "We will pass through Foggia." "You have any relatives there?" he asked. "No, but the famous Padre Pio is there." "Who's he?" asked my priest friend. "Oh, Jim," I said, "you've had your nose in philosophy books too long. The man I'm talking about has the wounds of Christ in his hands and side and feet." My friend was strangely unimpressed. The best response he could come up with was, "Well, I owe you one for putting up with my snoring." So we got off at Foggia, and conned an Italian cabdriver to take us to San Giovanni Rotundo and the Capuchin monastery there.

But when we told the brother who met us at the door that we had come to see Padre Pio, he said in disgust: (translation mine) "Oh, you Americans. Well, you cannot see Padre Pio." Then, in a moment of contrition, he added: "I can take you up to the room of Father Eustace. He handles all correspondence in English." So we wound up in the room of Father Eustace, who had been in Foggia for one year, having come from England. "Don't come here sniffing for miracles," Eustace warned us. "Get the man's doctrine, and you will be much better off," he wisely added.

But I had recently had the experience of meeting Helen Bradley, who was apparently cured of cancer by this mobile shrine of Lourdes. Contrary to the advice given us, I asked about the miracles. "Well," said Father Eustace, "he does seem to know everything. For example, I was vesting for Mass one morning and looked at the Ordo (the calendar of Feasts) and realized that my father had died in England five years ago on that date. I noticed Padre Pio was also vesting for Mass, so I went down to ask him to remember my father. I tapped him gently on the shoulder, and he turned to me with the words: "I have already prayed for your father."

Suddenly, we were interrupted by a loud banging on the door. It was again the brother who first admitted us: "Padre Pio is in the corridor with a doctor. If you hurry you can see him." We rushed out of the room of Father Eustace, who warned us that we should leave our cameras behind.

The brother again: "Padre Pio, there are two American priests here who wish to see you." Being Destiny's Darling, I was first in line. The saintly man held out his arms to give me an abrazzo (an embrace). He immediately began sniffing about me. "Where have you come from?" "From the Holy Land," I replied. "Oh, I thought I had detected the aroma of holiness about you." I turned to my friend, and told him to be sure to get down the exact time and place those words were spoken.

Padre Pio continued to joke with us for about fifteen minutes. I remember one joke he told. He asked us what we were studying in Rome. I said theology and he approved. My friend said philosophy and Padre Pio said it was always over his head. Most of the Roman people are called "Doctor" so Padre Pio told us of a man at a party who was introduced as "Doctor." A woman who was present heard this, and immediately began an "organ recital" of symptoms. "Excuse me, ma'am, but I am a doctor of philosophy, not medicine." The saintly Padre Pio turned up his face, and uttered the woman's response: "What can you possibly cure?" (funnier in Italian)

So we left Padre Pio, had supper, and then retired to our room. My friend the snorer was ready for bed, but wanted some photographs of Padre Pio, about whom he intended to write. A bit leery, I made him promise not to be asleep when I returned from the store.

So I went out on the streets of Foggia and noticed a sign: ABRESCH—Religious Goods. The metal protector for the storefront was only half drawn down, and so I stooped under it. There behind the counter was the prettiest Italian woman I have ever seen. She was saying her Rosary. I coughed, and without opening her eyes, she said: "One moment, Father." I remember thinking that everyone around this town knows everything.

Finished with her Rosary, the woman looked up at me and said: "Can I help you?" "Do you have a picture of Padre Pio?" I asked. She took me to a display and said, "You should be able to find here what you are looking for." I asked her if she knew Padre Pio personally, and she matter-of-factly replied: "He is my Spiritual Director." When I asked how all this came about, she said she was afflicted with a terminal disease. She told me how she had come from Turin to San Giovanni Rotundo, and how she had gone to confession to Padre Pio. He told her to lean out of the confessional, and "BOFFO (her word): he tapped my face." She wasn't cured until the next day. Weeks later, she was written up in *Newsweek* magazine, as a recent healing of Padre Pio.

Then she gave me the same advice as Father Eustace. "Don't be looking around for miracles. Get the man's doctrine." I admitted I was going to return to Rome the next day. She thought for a while, and then promised to remember me in her next confession to Padre Pio. "He always knows who it is that is being commended, and tells me how things will turn out. For example, I commend a member of my family, and he tells me that Mother will find the money she lost in a very short time. Or I say the same words of commendation about my sister and he tells me that the marriage my sister is thinking of entering into will not work out."

"So he will say something about me?" I inquired. "Yes!" came the reply. "And how will I know what he says?" I asked. "I will write it to you," she said. So I addressed and stamped an envelope to myself in Rome and told her to be sure to include everything that the Holy Man says. She promised she would. I paid for the pictures, and left.

When I returned to Rome, I did not get my envelope. So, at Christmastime I wrote to her, reminding her of her promise. She wrote back immediately (with my self-addressed envelope) and penned: "For the first time in ten years he said nothing. So I returned the next week and commended you under a different heading. For the second time in ten years, he said nothing. So I asked if he understood. 'Yes, I understand.' I don't know how to explain this."

When I had read her letter, I went to one of the leading mystical theologians in Rome, and asked for an interpretation. He said, "You are either too good to need a message or too bad to profit from one." Back on the horns of the dilemma.

So I wrote to Padre Pio himself. After asking to be included among his spiritual "bambini," I asked him if he had a message for me. I got a letter back from Father Eustace (even though I had written in Italian), saying that Padre Pio remembered me well, and that he would happily include me among his spiritual children. Finally, he had this message for me:

"If you make the will of God the center of your life, you will be happy."

(My reaction: Oh, I knew that.)

*T*he one who does God's will:
This person will enter the Kingdom.

Helen Bradley

I have told the story of my own encounter with Padre Pio. Now I would like to tell you about the encounter of Helen Bradley with Padre Pio.

My own mother was a schoolteacher in a high school in Chicago. One night she sadly announced that Helen Bradley, who taught at the same school, was dying of cancer. We all bowed our heads momentarily to remember Helen Bradley in our prayers.

About a month later, Mother made the surprise announcement that Helen Bradley had been cured miraculously. She was back teaching again. We didn't really understand, but were glad that Helen Bradley was well. I privately skimmed through a life of Padre Pio at the time, because my mother said that this Holy Man had prevailed upon God to work this miracle.

It seems that Helen Bradley was diagnosed with terminal cancer. She had the operations to cure the relentlessness of her disease, but in vain. Then she wrote to Padre Pio, asking his intervention in the matter.

One night she was quietly sitting with her sister, when the aroma of roses (Padre Pio's traditional sign) grew stronger and stronger. She asked her sister if she smelled anything. The sister denied that there was an aroma of any kind at all in the room. She said emphatically that she had spilled no perfume.

Then a friend came over, and Helen Bradley asked her the same question. The sister intervened. "The cancer has affected your sense of smell, Helen." The friend concurred. But Helen Bradley was quite sure that it was a sign from Padre Pio. She was sure she was "cured." So she went to her doctor and asked for another examination. The doctor was a bit perturbed by this, and told her, "Helen, go home, say your prayers and die." At this point Helen demanded another examination, and said she would pay for it herself. So the doctor acquiesced. He was amazed to find the cancer completely gone.

When Helen Bradley asked him to testify to the miraculous nature of her "cure," the doctor admitted that he did not believe in God. "I will testify that on this date you had terminal cancer, and on this later date that you have no cancer at all. How did it happen? Is it a complete remission? Is it faith? Will it last? I just do not want to postulate that God did this. I repeat: I just do not believe in God."

Years later, I said my first solemn Mass at St. Viator's Church in Chicago. A woman came up for my blessing at the reception later, and I did not recognize her. I asked who she was, and she said, "My name is Helen Bradley." "Helen Bradley, I've been waiting to meet you." She started to cry. "God has been very good to me," she said. I blessed her, and mused: "You have certainly blessed me."

I have chosen to give you my gift of love and you have chosen to love me.

108

My Priesthood Years

❧

As part of the ordination ceremony for the priesthood, those to be ordained prostrate themselves (signifying death to self) before the bishop. When finally the bishop asks who would be ordained the men arise in response, alive with the life of Christ Jesus, "Adsum." I secretly thought I would be transformed by this moment. I was disillusioned only minutes after the ordination ceremony when I became irritated by something. It was my old self that I thought had died at the altar of ordination.

The ensuing years were years of extreme busyness. Besides teaching (in Latin no less), if I had a free moment on my calendar of activities, I immediately filled it. Twenty-one books and probably a thousand public speaking lectures later I have come to the conclusion that I overextended myself. I guess I was still trying to die.

On this overcrowded schedule I would list The Fully Alive Experience as one of the most productive ventures. It was a three-day seminar for groups seeking personal and spiritual growth. We began giving this program in Australia and New Zealand (in case it didn't fly, we could fly home). Then we went to all fifty states in the United States to try our luck.

In Australia, there was a man in the audience who fixed us with a decidedly unfriendly face. It was not until the end of the FAE weekend that he approached us with the word that this had been the most life-transforming experience of his whole life. I tried to memorize his lines so that I would never forget that the real story of each person lies deep beneath the surface.

To return to my teaching, I originally was assigned to West Baden College to teach in our seminary there. That is when I taught in Latin. After seven years in seminary teaching, I was assigned to Loyola University to teach theology. I remained at this position for the next thirty years. Loyola became a home for me.

At one point when I was just about to give up teaching and turn my focus toward work in the media, I assigned the students to write "faith journals." Originally, the students were asked to respond to the forty questions at the back of my book, The Secret of Staying in Love. *I had very much enjoyed the "give and take" of the classroom, but I found a new dimension of my students in these "journals," which I read religiously. Here they opened up at much deeper levels to me and to themselves than they ever had in the classroom.*

Among other things I said in my written response to these journals was this: "Twenty years from now you will certainly wonder what you thought and how you felt while in college. These answers of yours that you've written will supply that information. The story of your life will gradually unfold and then you will be glad that you took the time and made the effort to write this part of your life story now."

As the recipient of these life stories I was abundantly graced. Each one of these journals taught me something special. And all of them taught me that every person, when understood, makes psychological sense. They may be different from me in some ways but all their parts taken together make sense for them. And what they need from me is not to rearrange their parts to suit me but simply to love them.

My First Retreat
to Priests

❧

It was my first retreat to priests. I got the letter of
invitation in the seminary where I was teaching, and
immediately fired off a response accepting the retreat.
When I arrived, the butterflies were only slightly active in
my stomach.

However, standing outside the chapel doors as the
priests filed in, I started to panic. I suddenly realized that I
would be the youngest man in the chapel. There were also
two bishops making the retreat. It almost seemed that
everyone was in a red cummerbund except me. Even the
monsignor greeting the priests at the doors of the chapel
was wearing a red cummerbund and a white lace surplice.
He asked me how I felt and I said: "Terrified."

He looked surprised. "Terrified. Why?" I replied, "Did
you see them? "Oh," he said in a way that I knew was
supposed to be comforting, "They just need what
everybody needs, a little love and a little understanding."
"Then, why don't they look like it?" I said as I followed the
retreatants into chapel.

We were trained to render the audience benevolent by
a little humor. But what do you do when no one laughs? In
fact, when I looked out at my priest retreatants, they all
had their arms folded in front of them. I had just finished

reading Julius Fast's book on body language, which said that when people fold their arms this way, they are saying: "You'll never get through to me." And that is the way this group of men looked to me.

In fact, the only time they laughed was when one of their number fell asleep. He snored like a dive bomber, and no one woke him up. He was bald, and I could see his bare scalp bobbing up and down before me.

As I walked out of the chapel, I promised myself that this was the last priests' retreat I would ever give. Why did I choose this form of martyrdom?

Then I walked quietly to the priest-retreat-master's room. There I heard chimes coming out of the closet. Lordy, that's all I needed. Chimes. So I opened the closet door, and discovered that it was a confessional. But who would possibly come to confession to me? I figured that it must be one of the sisters who took care of the retreat house.

But alas! It was a priest. In fact, five priests came to confession that first night. Three of them cried. Tears of disappointment, loneliness. I found myself taking back what I had promised myself about this being my final priests' retreat. I truly felt a compassion for them.

I have given a priests' retreat every year since then.

Many of life's greatest opportunities come into our lives disguised as problems.

One of Us Is . . .

❧

A group of monks living in a monastery were not getting along well. Their turbulent emotions often resulted in unkind words.

At the gate of the monastery was an old hermit, who had built his hermitage on the monastery grounds. The monks in the monastery, at their monthly meeting, decided to see if the ancient hermit could say something that would help them get along better.

So they elected their oldest member to approach the hermit. The elected monk was admittedly a bit shaky, but they said to themselves he would at least bring back the message without prejudice.

So the shaky old monk and the ancient hermit got together, and the monk told his story of mild dissension in the monastery. The ancient hermit stroked his long, white beard, and finally said:

"You may deliver my message only once, with no explanations. Those who wish to hear it will."

The message to the monks was this:

"You must try to see the Messiah in one another."

So the shaky old monk assembled all the monks in the whole monastery, and said that the hermit did have a message for the community. He told them that he was to say this only once with no explanation. So, drawing in a deep breath, he said:

"One of us is the Messiah!"

All dissension faded, and the monks got along very well from then on.

Jesus will live in each of the members of his Church.

Ray Charles on Blindness

Ray Charles is a blind pianist and vocalist. I saw an interview with him that is worth repeating. The interviewer asked: "I have heard it said that if God were to offer you your sight back, you would not take it. Is this true?" The pianist-vocalist admitted that this is true. He said, "When you can't see you just appreciate others more. Sometimes beautiful people enter one's life. They are not packaged very beautifully. But you don't know this when you are blind."

"When one of my children crawls into my lap, I just feel that there is someone there who loves me and whom I love. If I could see, I would probably see dirt on his clothes or shoes. And I would probably say: 'Go clean your clothes (or shoes) before you crawl into my lap.'

"I don't see that child as black or white, cleaned up or not cleaned up. I only feel that child as ninety pounds of love."

I probably wouldn't have remembered that interview if I had not been told myself by an eye doctor years ago: "You will probably be blind someday." In fact, I am now legally blind. I am already cherishing the little sight I have left. I try to memorize the sky, the leaves, the lakes, and I think of the day when these sights might be gone. I feel sad at this thought.

Then I remember Ray Charles.

"Lord, be merciful to those who travel by night."

It may be that God will make us uncomfortable until we say "yes."

Father Porcupine

I n the Society of Jesus, of which I am a member, we have all or most of the human types. The man whom I share about in this story was such a meanie we secretly called him Father Porcupine. I had taught with him prior to my own ordination, and somehow managed to stay at a safe distance during those three years.

But when it was announced that he was coming to live in the same building as I lived, I decided to go down and meet him. When I met him at the front door, I offered to carry his luggage to his room. "You didn't expect me to carry it, did you?" he rather caustically replied. So I picked up his luggage and brought him to the most spacious room in the building. (The building was erected about 1895.) "Bet the damned place is drafty," he lamented on entering the room. "Well, we have an excellent carpenter, who will be very happy to seal your windows, if you wish," I said.

He said, "S'pose you get up around here at some ungodly hour, like five in the morning." I tried to be as accommodating as possible: "Well, you came to relax, and so I can wake you about nine or ten and serve your Mass." I think his grunt was an agreement, so I took it as a yes.

When I entered his room the next morning between nine and ten o'clock, I immediately thought he looked like a beached whale. Then I proceeded to make my first mistake: I leaned over his sleeping form and said: "It's uppy uppy time!" If looks could kill, I wouldn't be writing this story. He had pure hatred in his eyes.

He struggled out of bed and admitted he had a great deal of difficulty getting his shoes and socks on. Since Tertianship is a year of spiritual training, I offered to do this for him, meanwhile thinking (only thinking): "I'll bet you haven't seen your knees for years, so large is your . . . protuberance."

Somehow, I managed his socks and shoes, and personally served his Mass. Each day his last words to me were, "I'll see you tomorrow at the same time." Omigosh!

So it became routine. (Except for "uppy uppy" time!) Pretty soon he moved out of the spacious room into a room next to mine on the third floor, "so you can type a few letters for me." I put on a new cap as typist and proofreader.

When my time was up, and I was leaving Tertianship for Rome, I said goodbye to Father Porcupine. He unashamedly embraced me and cried. I was secretly sorry that no other Jesuit saw this. No one would have believed it!

But now he is in heaven enjoying eternity, "if the damned place isn't drafty."

Listening is a searching to find the treasure of the true person.

Father Joe and The Franklin

❧

Joseph O'Callaghan wrote the book, *I Was Chaplain on The Franklin.* However, there is a story behind the story. Joe O'Callaghan was falsely accused by the navy. He inquired as to the source of his accusation, and was told that another chaplain had been his accuser. Unfortunately, Joe knew the man, and knew that he was not in control of his mind. He also knew that if he said anything to defend himself, the whole case would be investigated and the poor insane man would be court-martialed. So he said nothing.

Then the commander aboard the ship, *The Franklin,* asked the navy for a chaplain. He was about to set out on a dangerous mission. He received the reply: "We have no chaplain to offer you. We have only one priest in reserve, and he has a bad reputation." The commander of the ship called in: "Send him." So Joe O'Callaghan boarded the ship, and soon *The Franklin* set out.

The Franklin in its journey was torpedoed by the enemy. All the officers were killed, so the chaplain took over. At one point, a fire began raging on the deck. Joe O'Callaghan took a hose and was protecting the ammunition aboard the ship. The self-effacing chaplain had turned into a lion, a leader.

The Franklin was not sunk, and eventually limped into port. The chaplain, when his heroics were recorded, was awarded the Congressional Medal of Honor by the late President Truman. He was uncomfortable in the same room as praise, so he looked a bit embarrassed as the medal was hung around his neck.

When the war was over, Joe O'Callaghan returned to his position as professor of mathematics at Boston College. Later he had a debilitating stroke, and was confined to a wheelchair. He tried to keep up with all the new developments in mathematics. "You can never tell. I might recuperate and teach again."

Some years later, when the media belatedly heard of his heroics and the awarding of the Congressional Medal, they flocked to Boston College for a Joseph O'Callaghan interview. They asked him to pose with his medal. Suddenly, he looked a little uncomfortable. "I don't remember where I put it. I think I gave it to Father Minister or someone," he said. His values had survived with him.

The Angel of Death has now come to Joe O'Callaghan. Now he sees everything in perspective. He even knows where his Congressional Medal of Honor is.

*W*hen *Jesus enters a life, he transforms that life. He leads us in unpredictable ways to personal greatness.*

The Power of Expectations

M uch of what our lives turn out to be is based on our expectations. If we expect some rainy days, we will not be so disappointed when the sun doesn't shine. For example, a man drives home after a grueling day at the office, expecting that the children will all be properly bathed and dressed for dinner, which will be on the table. He is bound to experience some frustration when his expectations are not met.

Expecting that children will be perfect can be very disappointing. I read somewhere that the average child receives 431 negative messages every day. Now a negative message is not necessarily a scolding. "You're too small to reach that . . . Stop banging on the piano . . . Don't you know how to tie your shoes yet? . . . What do you mean, you need glasses? . . ."

These are only a few of the negative messages given to children every day. They can eventually result in a failure complex. I remember that one of my students said he was dropping out of school just before exams. When I asked him why he was dropping out now, he said: "If I say I 'dropped out' it is not as bad as saying I 'flunked out.' "

During my teaching years, when I had students write journals, I read every word of those journals. I tried in my comments to put together the pieces that had been torn apart. Not one of the many students whose journals I read had a superiority complex. Since then I have found that when I meet someone who seems to have a superiority complex it is actually an act put on to hide an inferiority complex.

On the college campus I saw a sign that read: "Expect a miracle." Keep your feet on the ground, but your head in the clouds. Life will probably turn out to be whatever you expect it to be.

The God who has touched me in the past will act again in my life. I will feel his finger and find him all over again.

Goodfinders

Some years ago, a group of researchers decided to study happiness in a purely scientific sort of way. So they picked out the 100 most happy and contented persons they could find. They interviewed these 100 happiest people and fed the interviews into computers, all in an effort to find what they might have in common. They were at first thrown off by the fact that 70 percent of these people came from small towns with populations under 15,000. It was only when they were ready to give up, they found that 100 percent of these people did have something in common. They were all classic "goodfinders." (The scientists had to make up a word to describe this quality.) They looked for what is good in themselves, in others, and in all the situations of life.

Anyway, one of the nearby universities was going to give me an honorary doctorate if I would give their commencement address. Naturally, I was quite willing to do this, to trade words for a doctoral degree. So I gave the commencement address on "goodfinders." I urged the senior class to become goodfinders, since I was sure they would be happier.

About two months later, I got a letter from one of those graduates. She said that her father had taken pictures all day long of the graduation ceremonies and the parties afterward, only to discover at the end of the day that there was no film in the camera.

After telling me this, she concluded: "I dare you to be a goodfinder, and locate some good in that."

I held her letter in my hands for a long time, and only then composed a reply. It went something like this.

"Think of the humility your father gained by this oversight. Here he was, the father of a university graduate, but unable to show pictures (they tell me that a picture is worth 1,000 words) because of an oversight on his part. And think of the marvelous opportunity on your part to accept his apology and to forgive him. Belated congratulations."

There is a promise in every problem, a rainbow after every storm, a warmth in every winter.

The Eagle's Egg

There is a story about an eagle's egg and an American Indian who found it. The story tells the plight of an American Indian who finds an eagle's egg on the ground, outside its nest. The Indian searches for but cannot find the nest. Eagles traditionally nest high up in trees.

So with the very best of intentions, the Indian puts the egg into the nest of a prairie chicken. There it hatches.

When the eagle comes out of the egg, it looks around to see what it is supposed to be doing. It sees the other prairie chickens rising a few feet above the earth, then cawing and clawing at the earth. So it does the same.

Near the end of its life it sees a bird proudly flying overhead. It asks in astonishment, "What is that?" One of the prairie chickens that is nearby says, "That, my friend, is an eagle, but don't ever think you can do what it does. Why, it flies right up into the sun. You're a prairie chicken like the rest of us."

The story ends sadly. The eagle dies thinking it is a prairie chicken.

Human beings are a lot like this. If we tell one another that we are prairie chickens, we will rise only a few feet above the earth. But if we tell a person that he is an eagle, why, he may fly right up into the sun.

We are like mirrors to one another.

Eleanor's Sign

❧

Eleanor Roosevelt, the wife of Franklin, our former president, had a sign in her office. She had been attacked and belittled on several counts. I am beginning to think that there is no thesis on earth without its opposition, no person on earth who does not receive criticism for something. Eleanor's sign read: "No one can make you feel inferior unless you give him or her permission!"

I think that the meaning of the sign is very important. Let me make a stab at this meaning. (I have been told that I have an amazing grasp of the obvious.)

If a person thinks of self as (somehow) inferior, then the remark, "You are (somehow) inferior," will resonate inside that person as recognition. On the other hand, if a person does not think of self as (somehow) inferior, then it will resonate inside that person as a misunderstanding. At most it will seem to be a false impression.

The same is true of "good . . . beautiful . . . kind . . . intelligent, etc." If a person thinks of self as endowed by God with goodness, beauty, kindness, intelligence, he or she will be able to interiorize compliments for such. If the person does not recognize these qualities in self, he or she will assume other motives for the compliments. At least such a person will scratch his or her head.

So, Eleanor's sign has great meaning for me. In order to be hurt (or helped), we must first give our permission to be hurt (or helped).

What do I see when I look through the lens of my attitude toward myself?

Two Old Priests

When I was a young seminarian, I remember going up to the infirmary one night (honestly, I don't remember *why*). As the Brother Infirmarian was tucking in two bedridden priests for the night, I was standing in the dark corridor, witnessing the whole scene.

As he tucked in the first priest, putting the blanket up under his chin, the old fellow responded angrily, "Get your face out of mine, Brother."

The poor brother went quietly to the next room, to tuck in the second priest for the night. The priest responded gratefully. "Oh, Brother, you are so good to us. Before I fall asleep tonight, I will say a special prayer just for you."

Standing in the darkened corridor, a sudden realization struck me. Someday, I would be one of those two old priests.

The full realization was this. I was right now practicing for that moment. When one gets old, habits take over. Old cranks practice all their lives at being cranky. Old saints practice all their lives at being holy.

As one of my fellow Jesuits now says of himself, "I am closer to the finish line than I am to the starting place." I myself know that whatever I am now is whatever I have practiced all my life to be.

Our todays will lie heavily upon our tomorrows.

Surprise at Stateville

❧

S ome years ago I wrote an article on taking responsibility for one's actions. An inmate at Stateville (the state prison in Illinois) started up a correspondence with me. He said he learned more from my article than from anything else. I was naturally flattered, so when he invited me to come visit with him in Stateville, I accepted the invitation.

I invited him eventually to write his life, but no publisher proved interested. One time when I was visiting him at the state prison, I met an old lady who was there to visit her nephew. She was so nice to everyone who encountered her that I was deeply impressed.

What added to my impression of this elderly woman was the atmosphere of distrust and violence seen at Stateville. Some of the criminals imprisoned there were led into sight with leather vests and their built-in handcuffs. These handcuffs were attached to beefy prison guards. The looks in the prisoners' eyes showed anger and violence as their eyes darted around.

One day on the pathway into the prison, I was side by side with the African-American lady who had so impressed me with her kindness. I couldn't really help myself as I said to her: "You must do a lot of good. You are so expressively kind to everyone you meet."

She said to me—and I had no reason to doubt that she
meant it—"Father, I greet no strangers but only brothers
and sisters whom I haven't yet met."

As I made my way through the atmosphere of distrust,
I reflected on this. This is what the Scriptures tell us, that
we are all brothers and sisters in the Lord. We are the sons
and daughters of God. And of all the places to realize this:
in Stateville.

*When God speaks, there will always be
something surprising, distinctive and lasting.*

The Hawthorne Sisters

O nce upon a time I was invited to give a retreat to the Hawthorne Dominican Sisters. I had known them well. The daughter of the legendary writer, Nathaniel Hawthorne, had founded this order of sisters. The other thing that was remarkable about them was that they nursed only indigent cancer victims. If a cancer victim had the funds to go elsewhere, that was where she was sent.

In preparing the retreat, I planned a strong emphasis on suffering, since the sisters saw only death. Death was all about them. They smelled death in the corridors. They were constantly on call for another victim. As a matter of fact, when I arrived at the convent, I was told that some of the sisters might be called from the conferences to attend to a dying person. Indeed they were.

What surprised me most about the sisters was their joy. The sisters had purchased an old hearse, which was painted over, and used to pick up their patients. I saw this hearse in action more than once. One of the younger sisters had learned to whistle loudly with two fingers in her mouth. It was a signal to the driver of the hearse. In a private conference I asked one of the sisters to explain to me why the sisters were so joyful. "You will have to ask our patients about that," she replied. "They are the source of our joy."

An incident happened just as I was nearing the end of the retreat, which helped me better understand their joy. I heard the whistle of the young sister. I saw the hearse pull out. The caller had said there was a woman lying on a pile of rags, who was dying of cancer. The sisters immediately swung into action.

The woman was picked up gently off her rags, brought to the convent, bathed, and clad in brightly colored silk pajamas. She was put to bed between immaculate white sheets, and ten minutes later she died.

"What a shame!" I said. "Oh no," replied one of the sisters. "That is what this is all about. She died with the dignity of a child of God."

I think I better understood their joy.

You are a real gift to this world and a person of inestimable worth.

The Lead Tenor

⌒∽⌒

I was in Rome, Italy, getting a doctorate in theology. I asked around about a place for my annual retreat and got the advice: Bad Schönbrun (a Jesuit retreat house) is the ideal place. It is high up in the Alps. Bad Schönbrun is in Switzerland and, strictly speaking, the Jesuits are not supposed to be there. Some decree of the Swiss government outlaws the presence of any Jesuit in Switzerland. Anyway, I wrote ahead to Bad Schönbrun and was accepted for my retreat.

The little bus chugged up the side of the Alps, at the top of which was a clearing. A German-speaking brother met me at the bus, and said: "Kommen sie zu Kapel. Wir singen." (Come to chapel. We're singing at Benediction.)

So off to chapel we went. While I fidgeted with the German language hymnal, I was surprised to hear one of the most beautiful voices I had ever heard. It was coming from a man standing directly behind me, and my mind was distracted from the Benediction by the melodiousness of this voice.

Benediction over. As we were walking out of the chapel, I sidled up to the man with the voice, and in my best German, I said: "Entschuldigen sie bitte, aber sie haben eine shone stimme." (Excuse me, please, but you have a beautiful voice.) At least that is what I intended to say. He was humbly grateful, and we struggled through about ten minutes of German conversation. By the way, I found the German language a bottomless pit. I was about to tell him that he should have his voice trained, but I couldn't think of the German word for "trained." Eventually, he presented his card. It read: "Walter Hegge, Lead Tenor of the Zurich Opera Company." (More footprints around my mouth.)

Finally, he said in English: "Is German your native language?" "No," I said with great relief, "I don't even speak English well, but it is my native language." At this point we were ready for a formal introduction, so I formally met "Walter Hegge," lead tenor of the Zurich Opera Company.

He invited me to take a walk up into the mountains after dinner. When I was assured that he did not mean mountain climbing, I accepted. As we walked up the path into the mountains, he told me his life story. God had pursued him from the days of his youth in South Africa and finally caught him on the stage in Zurich.

"And what are you doing here now, Walter?" "Oh, Father, I forgot the most important part of my story. I am going to be baptized on Sunday, and I am preparing for this great grace by a retreat."

We came to a log fallen across our path, and I immediately sat down on it, and said, "I am ready, Walter." "Ready for what?" he asked. "You are going to sing for me," I said. First, he started to walk back in the direction of the retreat house. I was certain he was going back for his music. In fact, he was sparing me the full force of his voice. Up close it could have blown me off the side of the mountain. As he sang, the small chalets which had closed their shutters for the night suddenly opened those shutters, and heads peered out as though perhaps Gabriel had at last blown the horn.

I made my retreat for the next eight days, but the sight of the Alps behind Walter Hegge, the story of his life and the beauty of his voice, the sight of the sun setting gently just behind my talented friend, stayed with me. Sights and sounds filled my imagination, as I sought to find the face of God in Bad Schönbrun.

The greatest gift of God is the gift of life.

Abba, Father

❧

I t appears from the Scriptures that God wants us to think of Him, to call Him "Our Father." I never really had an image for this or thought of God precisely in this way. Then I took a trip to the Holy Land, in search of (a father figure) the face of God.

It happened to me in Israel. A bus that I was riding on suddenly lurched, and a little boy who was playing in the aisle of the bus bumped his head.

Holding his hand over his bruised forehead, he went crying to his father. "Abba, I bumped my head." The father tenderly kissed the bump and held the little boy in his arms. The boy fell asleep there.

As I viewed the little boy in his father's arms, secure and asleep, the look of compassion and love on the father's face, I understood why God wants us to think of Him and to call Him "Abba," our Father.

God *is love!*

Ninth Inning

❧

I *n 1995, I retired from teaching at Loyola University in Chicago. I presumed I would do some more public speaking and continue writing. Though I had experienced some physical difficulties, I didn't expect that they would slow me down very much. Over the years, most people had experienced me as a person of boundless energy.*

In my youthful twenties I was diagnosed with a genetic condition called retinitis pigmentosa, *a gradual loss of peripheral vision. Since my original diagnosis, I hadn't really noticed much difficulty over the years. I figured I was one of the lucky ones. I have also had a few episodes with imbalance in recent years, but I was compensating well for that whenever it occurred. I was still swimming laps every day and going to the office to write.*

My unfortunate years were about to explode. My hearing began to fail. My hip needed replacing. I was told I had developed late-onset diabetes. Both the eyesight and imbalance worsened. One of the doctors I saw during this time said I had so many irons in the fire, they may have to create a new diagnosis called Powell's Syndrome.

During these difficult years, I received all the doctoring that was suggested and gratefully accepted all the help that was offered—just to keep going. I was still endowed with boundless energy. I don't think any of us ever stops thinking of ourselves as young. We think we're as young, as energetic and independent, as our imaginations tell us we are. Sooner or later, the picture and the reality don't even come close.

This happened for me in the year 2000. I realized it was time for me to accept the help available in an assisted-living center for Jesuits in Michigan. It's a wonderful place with loving and caring people and friends from all my early Jesuit years for good company. Even with all that going for it, it was hard for me to make the decision to leave Loyola, on whose doorstep I first arrived for high school when I was thirteen years old. And, of course, it was especially difficult to leave family and friends in Chicago. But the very hardest leave-taking of all has been to let go of my youthful self-impression and my independence.

For years I have counseled people with a paraphrase from Viktor Frankl: "Don't question life. Let life question you." So now I am taking my own counsel. These days as I enjoy my new home—and I do enjoy it—I ask God what this latest chapter in the story of my life has to teach me. I am beginning to see myself gradually returning to the first chapter of my life, but this time I am sitting in the lap of a trustful God. And I am listening to God's stories of how much we are loved throughout all the days of our lives.